ORTHO'S All About
Trees

Written by Jan Johnsen and John C. Fech

Meredith₀ Books
Des Moines, Iowa

Ortho® Books
An imprint of Meredith® Books

Ortho's All About Trees
Editor: Michael McKinley
Art Director: Tom Wegner
Copy Chief: Catherine Hamrick
Copy and Production Editor: Terri Fredrickson
Contributing Editors: Nancy Engel, Ed Malles
Contributing Technical Editor: Harrison L. Flint
Contributing Copy Editor: Martin Miller
Technical Proofreader: Mary Pas
Technical Photo Researchers: Cynthia Haynes,
    Leona Holdsworth Openshaw
Contributing Proofreaders: Kathy Eastman, Steve Hallam
Contributing Illustrator: Mike Eagleton
Contributing Map Illustrator: Jana Fothergill
Contributing Prop/Photo Stylists: Mary E. Klingaman,
    Diane Munkel Pamela K. Peirce
Indexer: Donald Glassman
Electronic Production Coordinator: Paula Forest
Editorial and Design Assistants: Kathleen Stevens,
    Karen Schirm
Production Director: Douglas M. Johnston
Production Manager: Pam Kvitne
Assistant Prepress Manager: Marjorie J. Schenkelberg

**Additional Editorial Contributions from
    Art Rep Services**
Director: Chip Nadeau
Designer: lk Design
Illustrators: Shawn Wallace, Vera Wong

Meredith® Books
Editor in Chief: James D. Blume
Design Director: Matt Strelecki
Managing Editor: Gregory H. Kayko
Executive Ortho Editor: Benjamin W. Allen

Director, Sales & Marketing, Retail: Michael A. Peterson
Director, Sales & Marketing, Special Markets:
    Rita McMullen
Director, Sales & Marketing, Home & Garden Center
    Channel: Ray Wolf
Director, Operations: George A. Susral

Vice President, General Manager: Jamie L. Martin

Meredith Publishing Group
President, Publishing Group: Christopher M. Little
Vice President, Consumer Marketing & Development:
    Hal Oringer

Meredith Corporation
Chairman and Chief Executive Officer: William T. Kerr
Chairman of the Executive Committee: E.T. Meredith III

On the cover: Japanese maple. Photograph by Janet
    Loughrey.

All of us at Ortho® Books are dedicated to providing you
with the information and ideas you need to enhance your
home and garden. We welcome your comments and
suggestions about this book. Write to us at:
    Meredith Corporation
    Ortho Books
    1716 Locust St.
    Des Moines, IA 50309–3023

If you would like more information on other Ortho
products, call 800-225-2883 or visit us at www.ortho.com

Thanks to
Phil Damner, Francesca Guiliani, Ian Harris, Cathy
    McReynolds, Ralph Notor

Photographers
(Photographers credited may retain copyright ©
    to the listed photographs.)
L= Left, R= Right, C= Center, B= Bottom, T= Top,
    i= Inset
William D. Adams: 69Ci, 72CR; **John E. Bryan:** 31CB, 75C; **David
Cavagnaro:** 53Ci (lower), 59C, 60BR, 68Bi (lower), 77C, 82T, 82Ti,
83T, 84Bi, 89T; **Walter Chandoha:** 4T, 4BR, 8BR, 15BR ; **Josephine
Coatsworth:** 58BR; **Crandall & Crandall:** 26C; **R. Todd Davis:** 54C,
56TLBR, 64T, 65Ti, 77Ci, 78Bi (left); **Joseph DeSciose:** 27TR, 69T;
Alan L. Detrick: 40BR; **Michael Dirr:** 19C Row 2, 23 Row 3-1&3,
42TL, 45BC, 45BR, 45BRi, 46TR, 47 Row 2-2, 48C, 49C, 50C, 51C,
52BL, 55Ci, 55B, 56TRRT, 56CLi, 57TR, 57C, 58C, 58Ci, 59Bi, 60Ti,
60BC, 62B, 63B, 65Ci, 65B, 71Ci, 75Ti, 75Ci, 76CL, 78B, 80Ti (two),
84B, 85Bi, 86Ti, 89B, 90CR, 92B; **Catriona Tudor Erler:** 18Ti, 23
Row 4-3, 53C, 76CR; **Derek Fell:** 5TL, 12TL, 12BL, 16, 17, 19CR,
31BR, 33BR, 47BR, 52Ti, 58T, 67Ti, 70TR, 70BC, 74TR, 81Ti, 86B,
89BL, 90T; **Charles Marden Fitch:** 19TL, 27BR, 61T, 68Ti (top), 75T,
75Bi, 87C; **Harrison L. Flint:** 5TR, 15TR, 20 Row 2-4, 23 Row 4-1,
53T, 53Ti, 55Bi, 69Bi, 72B, 73C, 73B, 74T, 74Ti, 79TLi, 80T, 82B,
82Bi, 83C, 83BL, 86Ci, 87T, 87Ti, 90B, 91C; **John Glover:** 18BL, 20TC,
20 Row 3-3, 21BC, 23 Row 4-2, 44, 45BL, 46CL, 47CT, 48T, 51Ci, 54B,
59T, 61BR, 62TL, 64Bi, 67B, 78T, 84T; **David Goldberg:** 15BL, 28TL,
35TR, 35BL, 37BR, 38TL, 38CL, 39TR, 39CR, 39BR; **Jeff Gracz:** 81T;
Pamela J. Harper: 19C Row 4, 49Ti, 51BL, 56CL, 56Bi (top), 57B,
62TLi (two), 66T, 68Ti (lower), 69Ti (lower), 82C; **Jerry Harpur:** 8T,
11, 78BLC, 88Ti; **Lynne Harrison:** 19C Row 5, 23 Row 1-2, 54T, 69C,
80B, 88Bi, 89Bi; **George M. Henke:** 22TR; **Horticultural Photography:**
24-25T, 46BL, 47 Row 2-3, 47BC, 50BL, 52T, 52BR, 55C, 56TRRB,
58BL, 59Ti, 60T, 65T, 66Ti, 68T, 73T, 74C, 74B, 77T, 77Ti, 81Bi, 92T;
Jerry Howard/Positive Images: 21TL, 22 Row 2-1, 25TR; **Bill Johnson:**
49Ci, 53Ci (top), 55Ti, 90CL, 91Ti; **Mark Kane:** 21TC; **Alan
Kearney/ENP Images:** 21TR; **Andrew Lawson:** 5BL, 18C, 50BR, 70TC,
72CL, 74Ci, 78C, 79BL, 85T, 88T; **Lee Lockwood/Positive Images:**
14T; **Janet Loughrey:** Cover, 19CRi; **Allan Mandell:** 10T, 25BR, 26T,
71TR; **Charles Mann:** 49Bi, 77Bi, 89C; **Stuart McCall:** 66C; **Bryan
McCay:** 34, 39BC, 42BL; **David McDonald/PhotoGarden:** 68B, 79TL;
Michael McKinley: 8BL, 12TR, 13TL, 13BL, 13BR, 32TR, 32BL, 33TR;
Rick & Donna Morus: 48B, 68Bi (top); **Clive Nichols:** 5BR, 21CR, 22
Row 3-1, 23 Row 2-2&3, 48Ti, 54Ti, 61BC, 67T, 79BR; **Stephen G.
Pategas:** 29BR ; **Jerry Pavia:** 7, 12BR, 27BL, 45CR, 74Bi; **Ben
Phillips/Positive Images:** 20 Row 2-2, 23 Row 3-2; **Cheryl R. Richter:**
22 Row 2-3, 23BR, 26B; **Susan A. Roth:** 4BL, 6, 10B, 13TR, 18TL,
19TC, 20 Row 3-4, 21BR, 22 Row 2-2, 22 Row 3-4, 23 Row 2-1, 24TL,
46TL, 55T, 56B, 56TRL, 56Bi (lower), 61BL, 62C, 64B, 66BL, 66Bi,
66BR, 69Ti (top), 69B, 70BR, 71C, 75B, 77B, 78Ci, 79TR, 79TRi, 80C,
80Ci, 81B, 83BR, 85C, 85B, 87B, 88C, 91T, 92C; **Richard Shiell:** 19TR,
19C Row 3, 21CL, 22 Row 2-4, 22 Row 3-3, 23 Row 1-1, 50T, 52CR,
54Ci, 57Bi, 61Ti, 63T, 64Ti, 67C, 67Ci, 67Bi, 70CC, 70TRi, 71B, 72T,
72Ci, 76T, 76Ti, 76B, 79BLi, 80Bi, 83Ci, 86T, 86Bi, 88B, 91Ci, 91B ;
Holly H. Shimizu: 51T; **Pam Spaulding/Positive Images:** 19BR, 20 Row
3-2; **Guy & Edith Sternberg:** 51BR, 53B, 59B, 64C, 86C; **The Studio
Central:** 28TR; **Michael S. Thompson:** 14B, 18Ci, 18Bi, 20TR, 20 Row
2-1, 20 Row 2-3T, 20 Row 2-3B, 20 Row 3-1, 21BL, 22 Row 3-2, 23 Row
1-3, 43BR, 46BLi, 49B, 52CL, 56TL, 56TLBL, 58BL, 60BL, 65C, 71Bi,
88Ci; **Connie Toops:** 48Ci, 53Bi; **judywhite/New Leaf Images:** 31TC,
47TR; **Wolf Von dem Bussche:** 49T

THE RIGHT TREE FOR THE PURPOSE 4

The Value of Trees **4**
Make Your Yard More Comfortable **6**
Shape Outdoor Space **8**
Compose a Beautiful Landscape **10**
Establish a Sense of Place **12**
Fast-Growing Versus Permanent **14**

THE RIGHT TREE FOR THE EFFECT 16

All-Star Trees **16**
Showy Flowers **18**
Showy Summer Foliage **20**
Showy Fall Foliage **21**
Late-Season Display **22**
Evergreens **24**

THE RIGHT TREE FOR THE PLACE 26

Region and Zone **26**
Soil, Light and Air **28**
Analyzing Your Site **30**
Tree Habitats **31**
Small-Space Trees **32**

PLANTING AND CARE 34

Acquiring Trees **34**
Planting New Trees **36**
After Planting **38**
Caring for a New Tree **39**
Pruning **40**
Caring for Established Trees **42**

TREE SELECTION AND GROWING GUIDE 44

THE RIGHT TREE
FOR THE PURPOSE

THE VALUE OF TREES

Trees have layers of meaning and of use. Their impact on the landscape transcends their size and stature. Trees root us in place with their continuity; they assure us that what has been before us will be here long after. They bring communities together in neighborhood plantings and in lightings of the town tree at Christmas. We plant trees in memory of our friends and family—they link us with our past. They mark the seasons of our year and are companions, lasting for lifetimes, generations, and millennia.

Our landscapes, when planted with trees, become more comfortable; we're shaded in summer and protected from winter winds. Trees structure outdoor space and shape it into rooms and hallways; their trunks are walls, their spreading boughs are ceilings. Like living works of art, they add color, form, and allegory to our gardens. And don't forget that trees are fun: In a child's heart, no play equipment will ever replace a good old climbing tree or rope swing.

From majestic beauty to sheer fun, trees are a landscape investment for a lifetime.

HOW TO USE THIS BOOK

This book will guide you on your quest to find the right tree, and help you care for and protect the trees you have. In the first chapter, we introduce you to design considerations that explain the hard work trees can perform in your landscape: how trees can make outdoor living more comfortable, how trees can shape your yard into usable space, how to combine trees for beautiful visual effect and style, and some tips on achieving the most rapid results.

The second chapter celebrates the showy effect that many trees offer with the changing seasonal drama of flowers, fruit, fall foliage and winter sculpture.

The third chapter will help you choose and place trees in the right location for their best health and most successful growth. Here we guide you through regional considerations as well as the particulars of your yard regarding soil, light, and microclimates.

The fourth chapter leads you through acquiring, planting and caring for new trees, as well as pruning techniques and care for established trees that you might already have.

The final chapter is a selection and growing guide to over 150 of the best trees for North American gardens.

TREES CAN INCREASE PROPERTY VALUE NOW

Their physical, aesthetic, and spiritual benefits are huge, but trees have material benefits, as well. Studies have shown that trees can increase the value of residential property by as much as 27 percent. Many top varieties mature slowly and can take years to reach their prime. Nonetheless, there are steps you can take right now to reap the benefits of trees today. According to the National Arbor Day Foundation, these six steps immediately affect property value:
- Protect existing trees during construction.
- Transplant trees from elsewhere on the property to the front lawn.
- Plant saplings on a future building site.
- Place a few large trees from a nursery to beautify or increase energy conservation.
- Encourage planting of street trees in newly developed areas.
- Prune off dead or dying branches in yard and street trees.

(For more on achieving rapid effects with trees, please turn to pages 14 and 15.)

If you need an appraisal for a specific tree, consult a trained tree appraiser, or contact the Council of Tree and Landscape Appraisers, 1250 Eye Street N.W., Suite 500, Washington, DC 20005.

IN THIS CHAPTER

The Value of Trees 4
Make Your Yard More Comfortable 6
Shape Outdoor Space 8
Compose a Beautiful Landscape 10
Establish a Sense of Place 12
Fast-Growing Versus Permanent 14

European beech 'Roseo-marginata'

Goldenchain tree

Japanese maple 'Osakazuki'

Korean stewartia

MAKE YOUR YARD MORE COMFORTABLE

This hedge of Japanese cedar and Leyland cypress effectively blocks wind for a distance of up to twice its height. Leyland cypress makes an especially rapid evergreen windbreak, growing up to 3 feet each year. Eventually it can reach a height of 75 feet or more.

Trees keep us comfortable. They shade us in the summer, act as windbreaks, clean pollutants from the air, and buffer noise. Not all trees provide the same benefits, of course, but plant the right tree in the right location, and you can create a comfortable place for outdoor living, reduce your heating and cooling costs, enjoy clean, fresh air, and have a beautiful garden as well.

DEFLECT WIND

You can reduce your annual heating bill by up to 20 percent if you plant a windbreak on the windward side of your house to deflect prevailing winter winds. Evergreen trees, with low-growing branches and dense winter foliage, are the best choice. For maximum protection, the trees should be planted close together, and they should be located no farther than twice their mature height from the house. Remember that snowdrifts develop on the downwind side, so plant trees a good distance away from driveways and walks.

BEST EVERGREEN TREES FOR A WINDBREAK

White fir (Abies concolor)	Norway spruce (Picea abies)	Scotch pine (Pinus sylvestris)
Leyland cypress (Cupressocyparis × leylandii)	Colorado spruce (Picea pungens)	Douglas fir (Pseudotsuga menziesii)
Eastern red cedar (Juniperus virginiana)	Austrian pine (Pinus nigra)	
	Eastern white pine (Pinus strobus)	

COOL THE AIR

Trees are efficient at cooling the air. Working somewhat like an evaporative air conditioner, a tree pumps water vapor from its leaves (a process called transpiration), and the air cools as the moisture evaporates. This is why it feels cool and fresh under a tree even on a hot day. The combination of shade and transpiration can reduce temperatures by 5° to 9° F.

CLEAN THE AIR

Like living filters, trees are nature's purifiers. Through openings (stomates) in their leaves, trees absorb pollutants. Each leaf dissolves sulfur and nitrogen, breaks down ozone, and metabolizes other compounds so the tree can use them. After processing all the chemicals, trees give off water and oxygen.

The combined chemistry of the thousands of leaves on each tree eliminates an enormous volume of pollutants from the air. The U.S. Forest Service estimated that in one year, the trees growing in the city of Chicago removed 6,145 tons of air pollutants. Trees also physically remove particles like soot and dust from the atmosphere. The particles stick to leaves and are washed away by rain.

REDUCE NOISE

Though it's a quality often overlooked, trees have an impressive ability to muffle noise. Their leaves and small branches act as baffles, absorbing and deflecting sound. You'll get maximum noise protection from a tree with dense leaves, not an open, lacy-leaved variety.

A combination of evergreens, deciduous trees, and dense shrubs is the best sound-absorption solution. For best results, trees and shrubs reaching at least 15 feet high should be spaced closely together in a bed at least 15 feet deep. Planting on a raised bed, high mound, or berm helps to deflect sound overhead as well as add the additional barrier of soil.

IMPROVE SOIL

Even below the ground, trees are doing beneficial things for the landscape. Tree roots anchor the tree in the ground and soak up water and nutrients from the soil. Root systems also prevent soil from eroding. They support an underground universe of beneficial insects and microorganisms. These, in turn, keep all the soil around them healthy and teeming with life. Some tree roots (such as honey locust, Japanese pagoda tree, and alder) even "fix" nitrogen into the soil, actually adding to its fertility.

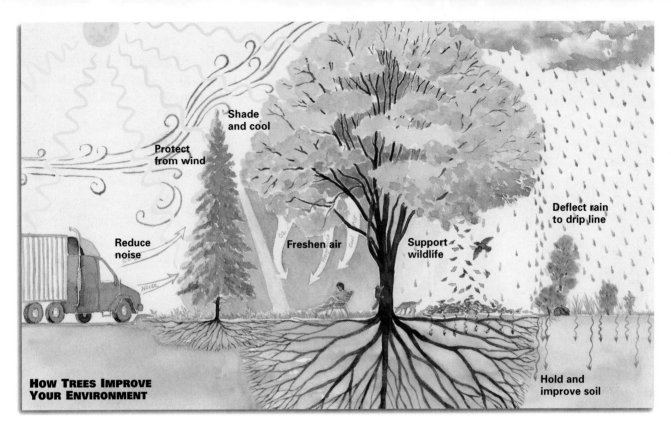

Shade and cool

Protect from wind

Reduce noise

Freshen air

Support wildlife

Deflect rain to drip line

Hold and improve soil

HOW TREES IMPROVE YOUR ENVIRONMENT

BEST TREES TO GROW FOR SHADE

Norway maple
(*Acer platanoides*)

Red maple
(*Acer rubrum*)

Silver maple
(*Acer saccharinum*)

Sugar maple
(*Acer saccharum*)

Horsechestnut
(*Aesculus spp.*)

Yellowwood
(*Cladastris lutea*)

Gum tree
(*Eucalyptus spp.*)

European beech
(*Fagus sylvatica*)

Sweet gum
(*Liquidambar styraciflua*)

Tulip tree
(*Liriodendron tulipifera*)

Plane tree
(*Platanus spp.*)

White oak
(*Quercus alba*)

Northern red oak (*Quercus rubra*)

Redmond linden
(*Tilia × flavescens* 'Redmond')

A well-placed shade tree can make even a small patio into a rich retreat.

WHERE TO PLANT A TREE FOR MAXIMUM SHADE

Both deciduous trees (those that lose their leaves each year) and evergreens (those which keep their leaves) provide shade. But you'll get maximum shade in the summer and maximum winter sun from a tall deciduous tree with a broad canopy of dense leaves. The temperature beneath a leafy tree can be 8° F cooler than in the open, and this cooling can be passed on to the inside of your house. By reducing the hot sun against your house, your cooling bills are reduced as well. For the most effective shading, place trees on the southwest, west, or northwest sides of the area or building to be shaded. These are the sides where the hot afternoon sun strikes in summer. The sun is highest in the early afternoon, so plant the tallest trees on the southwest side. Three well-placed shade trees can reduce your cooling costs by 35 percent.

SHAPE OUTDOOR SPACE

An outdoor room can be every bit as intimate and welcoming as any room in the house.

The lovely view of the water and boathouse is even better when framed by trees.

Trees are the bones of any design; they shape spaces and add structure like nothing else. Your first step toward a great garden is analyzing your space; your second step is defining it.

ENCLOSURE: To unify an open area, first enclose it. Think of it as putting up walls. A large, open lawn becomes a welcoming space when bordered by trees. The classic choice for this is evergreens, which have the added plus of working year-round, but you can use a mixed border or even a staggered grove of trees to get the same effect but with less of a solid feeling.

When you enclose your garden, you'll also gain privacy, and shape your view out of the yard. Eyesores are easily hidden by trees.

Once you've created the larger space, break it up into smaller spaces, into outdoor rooms. These smaller rooms invite visitors to sit and stay awhile. They create private spaces within your landscape. Make the walls of the rooms as solid or as light as you want, and in and around these rooms, plant shade trees for a roof or a ceiling.

MOVEMENT: Trees are crucial to guiding traffic within and among these rooms. They can welcome people into the backyard, announce the entrance to a garden room, or tie the house and yard together.

In a larger sense, trees create corridors and avenues within the garden. These can be formal or informal, dense, or airy, but they will guide movement, so take advantage of this. Use them to show off special plantings or favorite areas.

DRAMATIC VIEWS: The corridors and rooms you've created to this point are natural settings for your favorite garden views. If you're especially proud of a particular tree, design a room around it or with a great view of it. Elegant columnar trees can show off a favorite vista as well as any picture frame. Use your most spectacular trees at the end of corridors, and they will draw attention. And don't forget the views from your house; plan your more dramatic plantings with an eye toward the view from the house.

EXPANSION: If your space begins to feel cramped, there are ways to expand it. Make a space under the canopy of a tree to create a room without walls. Use perspective; with larger trees planted close and smaller ones farther away, the space will feel larger than it is. Or treat the garden as an expansion of the house, and it will make the house seem that much larger.

This allée of birches directs the eye exactly where the homeowner wants (right).

1. Define Boundaries
Enclosure can be as solid as a dense wall of evergreens or as suggestive as a single tree. Trees in staggered groves contain space while retaining openness.

2. Block Views
Trees can protect your privacy and screen unsightly views. Such screens are usually walls of thick foliage.

3. Develop Corridors
The trunks and foliage mass of trees direct traffic and connect garden rooms together. Passageways can be wide and sweeping, or narrow and intimate. They can be straight and direct, or meandering and full of mystery.

4. Set Focal Points
A tree with an unusual sculptural frame, or seasonal color, draws the eye like a magnet. Tall, narrow trees attract attention from a distance like exclamation points. Up close such columnar trees direct the gaze skyward. Use focal points with care; too many can simply confuse.

5. Enclose Intimate Rooms
Large properties can be made more intimate by dividing space into rooms. The connections between rooms become points of interest, and they encourage movement and exploration.

6. Establish Gateways
The trunks of trees establish gateways and portals between different parts of the yard. Areas between garden room and corridor, between the house and the yard, and between the private backyard and the public front yard, are all places for special treatment.

7. Spread Canopies Overhead
A canopy overhead not only protects from hot sun and rain, it provides its own sense of enclosure and intimacy—a garden room without walls.

8. Extend the Indoors Out
Trees arching over both house and yard create transitional spaces that extend indoor rooms out into the yard.

9. Frame Views
As with a painting, looking through a frame sets off a view and magnifies its effect. A view out a window can be enhanced with a frame as simple as a single tree trunk to one side.

10. Expand Sense of Space
Placing large, overscaled trees up close and smaller trees farther away increases the sense of depth and distance.

COMPOSE A BEAUTIFUL LANDSCAPE

Trees provide the basic structure and mass of the landscape. And the shapes of the trees are vitally important to this. When seen from a distance, such as from the street, the mass and skyline of the trees in your yard give your landscape weight and form. Rounded and spreading trees provide a horizontal mass that extends the house out, while the vertical mass of columnar and pyramidal trees extends your house upwards.

Overhead, the leafy canopy of spreading trees frames the view below it; the verticality of columnar trees lifts up the view almost like a tall window. Repeating these forms intensifies the effect, and varying them creates a dynamic, changing impression.

At eye level, tree trunks can frame a view, extend the vertical lines of the house into the landscape, or send the eye off through the mysterious depths of a grove. When repeated, these trunks establish rhythms, calming if repeated uniformly and more dynamic if interspersed with different shapes. Showy trees, or trees with unusual form, interrupt such a rhythmic path most especially and should be used sparingly.

Especially showy trees, such as this Japanese maple in full fall glory, make excellent accents to draw and arrest the eye.

The visual frame created by two tree trunks can be most effective when staggered, with one trunk closer to the viewer than the other. Such an arrangement creates added depth.

THE SHAPES OF TREES

Classifying the myriad shapes and sizes of trees into a few general forms helps us to combine trees in a landscape that is unified and pleasing to the eye.

ROUNDED AND OVAL TREES offer a regular shape that is ideal for a formal statement in rows and grids. Use them to create an effective corridor flanking a drive or street. Planted alone out in an open yard, they tend to achieve their most perfect, regular form. But in groups of three or more, their tops create a billowing mass of foliage very pleasing from a distance.

SPREADING TREES provide a horizontal reach that is very useful for continuing the horizontal lines of the house out into the landscape. These are the trees to choose when you are looking for a canopy over a patio or sitting area. And their overarching branches are perfect to establish a powerful frame for a favorite view.

PYRAMIDAL TREES have crowns that taper toward the sky; when seen from a distance, they tend to lift the eye upward. They can be cone-shaped evergreens, such as spruce and fir, or deciduous trees. Pyramidal greenspire lindens or scarlet oaks are as well suited for street tree plantings as for dramatic contrast behind rounded and spreading trees.

COLUMNAR OR FASTIGIATE TREES have a narrow, vertical form. They make dramatic sentinels that attract attention from a distance, and lift the eye upward like an arrow pointed to the sky. Their narrow diameter makes them a favorite for planting in colonnades, as screens and windbreaks, and to create garden rooms with walls of foliage. Many common tree species are available in this form.

MULTIPLE-TRUNK TREES lend the effect of a natural grove with a single specimen, while a modest planting of only three or five can create the feeling of an entire forest. Their frequently striking form makes them useful as an accent in more natural landscapes. And because they tend to arch out, they are often used at the corner of a house to soften its lines.

WEEPING TREES are the ideal accent to command attention in an important spot and seem especially fitting and effective next to water. A weeping cherry, for example, is a spectacular living sculpture. It makes a beautiful adornment for a pool or other small water feature.

The elegant, muscular trunks of European hornbeam are ideal for this formal, double colonnade, although they must be pruned frequently to remove lower growth. Repeating trunks in such a formal pattern is soothing and conducive to a meditative stroll.

10 BEST COLUMNAR TREES

Columnar red maple
(*Acer rubrum* 'Columnare')
Goldspire sugar maple
(*Acer saccharum* 'Goldspire')
Columnar European hornbeam
(*Carpinus betulus* 'Columnaris')
Columnar European beech
(*Fagus sylvatica* 'Fastigiata')
Ginkgo or maidenhair tree 'Princeton Sentry'
(*Gingko biloba* 'Princeton Sentry')
Crabapple 'Centurion', 'Sentinel', 'Red Baron'
(*Malus* 'Centurion', 'Sentinel', or 'Red Baron')
Columnar Sargent cherry
(*Prunus sargentii* 'Columnaris', 'Spire')
Amanogawa Japanese flowering cherry
(*Prunus serrulata* 'Amanogawa')
Callery pear 'Capital' or 'Chanticleer'
(*Pyrus calleryana* 'Capital' or 'Chanticleer')
Bald cypress 'Shawnee Brave'
(*Taxodium distichum* 'Shawnee Brave')

10 BEST WEEPING TREES

Laceleaf Japanese maple
(*Acer palmatum dissectum*)
Weeping Katsura tree
(*Cercidiphyllum japonicum* 'Pendula')
Weeping European beech
(*Fagus sylvatica* 'Pendula')
Red Jade crabapple
(*Malus* 'Red Jade')
Weeping Serbian spruce
(*Picea omorika* 'Pendula')
Weeping Yoshino cherry
(*Prunus* × *yedoensis* 'Shidare-yoshino')
Weeping Higan cherry
(*Prunus subhirtella* 'Pendula')
Weeping willow
(*Salix babylonica*)
Weeping Japanese snowbell
(*Styrax japonicus* 'Pendula' ('Carillon'))
Weeping Canadian hemlock
(*Tsuga canadensis* 'Sargentii')

ESTABLISH A SENSE OF PLACE

THEME AND STYLE

The personal expression possible with your home landscape is downright fun—and the place to start is with trees. Consider creating a prehistoric "forest primeval" in your own backyard with gigantic-leaved, "dinosaur-food" trees like bigleaf magnolia and empress tree, and the dramatic fluted trunks of dawn redwood. Or imagine a modernist formal grid with a canopy of white-leaved variegated boxelder and black-leaved Schwedler Norway maple overhead—and a carpet of bright red annuals underneath. From dwarf-tree gardens for model trains to Hansel-and-Gretel forest glades dripping with willows and romance, the possibilities for themed effects with trees are limited only by your imagination.

REGIONAL FIT

Successful landscapes balance personal expression with style appropriate to your region, your neighborhood, and the architecture of your home. A Japanese garden may be perfectly appropriate in the woodland context of the Pacific Northwest or the Atlantic Northeast, but seem jarring and out of place in the arid Southwest. Italian or Spanish garden styles are most appropriate when you have the architecture to match.

Using trees native to your area is a powerful technique to connect your property to its surrounding context. While native trees are ideal to create natural-appearing landscapes, like any tree they can be used just as well to create formal effects.

A traditional formal garden in the Northeast (above) features clipped hedges and a symmetrical design. An informal woodland garden in the same region (below) uses similar plants to idealize the forest understory.

A French formal landscape (above) with sheared hedges and rigid symmetry beautifully frames California's Napa Valley. A garden in the same region (below) celebrates a natural Mediterranean style with drought-tolerant plants.

TREES FOR FORMAL STYLE

The formal-versus-informal debate stretches back in history to the very origin of the landscape garden. Formal landscapes are marked by deliberate symmetry and strong, linear geometry. Frequently they incorporate trees almost as architecture, pruned into rectilinear hedges, topiary, and regular, geometric shapes such as spheres and obelisks. Basic elements of a formal garden include the allée (a straight corridor of trees converging on a focal point), the parterre (a four-square division of hedges), and the grid (a rectilinear planting of trees to create a formal grove). Trees favored in formal landscapes for their regular form include oval-form trees such as European hornbeam and callery pear, as well as rigidly columnar trees such as Italian cypress, columnar English oak, and some cultivars of American arborvitae.

TREES FOR INFORMAL STYLE

While formal gardens are experiencing a marked increase in popularity today, the informal garden style still captures the imagination of most people as it has for the past hundred years. Informal gardens are marked by flowing curves, assymetrical balance, and loose edges intended to create a naturalistic effect. Rather than replicate nature, the most successful informal gardens idealize it, selecting and concentrating the most beautiful trees into picturesque views. Some informal landscapes incorporate the many first-class trees native to the United States. Others successfully use the full palette of trees available from similar regions around the world to create seemingly naturalistic effects. A woodland glade in the Pacific Northwest, for example, would seem incomplete without Japanese maples.

This South Carolina formal garden (above) uses trimmed boxwood and small trees planted in a grid. In an Atlanta garden (below), boxwood has been allowed to grow in its natural form to match its forest surroundings.

An allée of native birches will handle the climate of the upper Midwest while still creating a strongly formal effect (above). An idealized woodland glen in Wisconsin (below) shows off the beauty possible with native plants.

FAST-GROWING VERSUS PERMANENT

To many gardeners, waiting for trees to grow is frustrating. Trees just don't grow "fast enough." You may be patient, but still not want to wait 30 years for a shade tree. Fortunately, there are several remedies.

A large, mature tree can create an immediate effect, but only at a great expense; a group of young trees creates a similar effect, but costs much less and often has better success.

TEMPORARY TREES give the fastest effect for your buck. Many will seem to spring up overnight, filling space very quickly. That's the good news. The bad news is that almost all of these trees have problems—they are weak-wooded, or they throw lots of litter, or have numerous pests. If you try one of these, be aware of its problems and be prepared to deal with the expense of having it removed (which can sometimes be quite expensive).

GROVES AND GROUPS of small trees can create a fast, strong effect. You should only use trees which do this in nature (others will not grow properly), such as birches. You can even combine fast growers with slower growers that are shade tolerant—over time the slower trees will replace the faster ones. This option is not without its dangers, though. The top growth of trees planted in groups adjusts to its situation; that is, it grows differently than if the tree was freestanding. So, if you thin the group later, the upper part of the trees will look odd. And also, as mentioned before, the expense and trouble of removing trees later is not to be taken lightly.

MATURE TREES are the fastest option. What could go wrong with buying an already mature tree? Plenty. Besides being very expensive, mature trees also don't take planting shock very well, and they run the risk of dying in the process. And even if they do survive, it might take them a few years to get back to a healthy, growing state. In those few years, smaller trees might have already caught up to them.

GIVING OPTIMUM CARE to the trees you really want is a good option. Many trees, when kept pest free and disease free, sited correctly, watered regularly, and mulched properly, will respond with faster-than-average growth. With such care, a good slow-growth-rate tree will grow at its best rate. This is not a cure-all or guarantee, however; while it works much of the time, the results, especially with naturally slow-growing trees, are not usually dramatic.

THE BEST SOLUTION borrows a little from all of these strategies. First, pick the highest quality, medium-to-fast growing trees that fit your needs and wants. Then give them the best site for their needs and follow up with the best care you can give. Plant them carefully, tend them regularly, and pay attention to them year-round. Watch for pests and signs of disease; water them correctly and deeply; mulch their root zone. This way, you get a quality tree, and more than likely, a good, fast effect in your landscape.

FASTEST-GROWING "TEMPORARY" TREES

Boxelder
  (*Acer negundo*)
Silver maple
  (*Acer saccharinum*)
European black alder
  (*Alnus glutinosa*)
Leyland cypress
  (*Cupressocyparis* ×
  leylandii)
Royal paulownia
  (*Paulownia tomentosa*)
White poplar
  (*Populus alba*)
Lombardy poplar
  (*Populus nigra* 'Italica')
Willows
  (*Salix* spp.)
Green Giant arborvitae
  (*Thuja* 'Green Giant')

TREES WITH MEDIUM-TO-FAST GROWTH RATE

Red maple
  (*Acer rubrum*)
Heritage river birch
  (*Betula nigra* 'Heritage')
Green ash
  (*Fraxinus pennsylvanica*)
Thornless honey locust
  (*Gleditsia triacanthos* var.
  inermis)
London plane tree
  (*Platanus acerifolia*)
Pin oak (*Quercus palustris*)
Northern red oak
  (*Quercus rubra*)
Coast redwood
  (*Sequoia sempervirens*)
Bald cypress
  (*Taxodium distichum*)
Chinese elm
  (*Ulmus parvifolia*)

PLANT FOR POSTERITY

No discussion of trees would be complete without acknowledging their tremendous lifespans. Some are nature's monuments, awesome not only in proportion but also in longevity. California sequoias (redwoods) often live over 2,000 years. The bristlecone pines in the southwest mountains are the oldest living trees in the world, approaching 5,000 years old. Trees are increasingly a symbol of endurance in our fast-paced, disposable culture.

If you want to plant a tree for your great-grandchildren, choose a long-lived genus like the oak. Here's an old English adage: An oak takes "300 years growing, 300 years standing still, and 300 years dying." The Middleton Oak in Charleston, South Carolina, bears that out—it's 900 years old. The Bedford Oak in Bedford, New York, was alive when our Constitution was signed. Oaks (white, live, and English) and beeches (American and European) are trees for legacies. So are horsechestnut, London plane tree, and sequoia. Plant these long-lived individuals in a wide-open area where they can grow unhindered for generations.

TREES TO PLANT FOR POSTERITY

Heritage river birch
  (*Betula nigra*
  'Heritage')
Gum tree (*Eucalyptus*)
Thornless honey locust
  (*Gleditsia triacanthos*
  var. *inermis*)
Tulip tree
  (*Liriodendron tulipifera*)

London plane tree
  (*Platanus acerifolia*)
Sargent cherry
  (*Prunus sargentii*)
Red oak
  (*Quercus rubra*)
Bald cypress
  (*Taxodium distichum*)

Sharing the planting of a tree ties generations together like few other acts. The young tree is in the here and now, but will also be here tomorrow and for generations to come. Even the most humble seedling can one day grow to become a magnificent tree.

THE RIGHT TREE
FOR THE EFFECT

The previous chapter explored the more permanent structural value of trees in the landscape. But many trees also offer short-term yet spectacular seasonal effects that provide a constantly changing drama around your home. Some trees drape themselves with beautiful flowers in spring or summer. Others provide attractive fruit in late summer and autumn, or burst into flaming foliage colors in fall. Still others come into their greatest glory after leaves drop to reveal startling sculptural form and beautiful bark.

Of course, a number of trees offer a colorful show over a very long season. Many cultivars selected for brightly colored leaves, such as red-leaved Japanese maple or white-and-pink-variegated dogwood, provide summer-long color as effective as any flowering tree. And a wide range of evergreens offers such colorful foliage all year long.

ALL-STAR TREES

Selecting trees that provide showy, changing effect in not just one but two or more seasons is an excellent way to pack the most colorful punch into your landscape and get the most bang for your buck. Such hardworking, multiple-season trees are relatively rare in the horticultural world; we call them "All-stars."

Billows of white, apple-like blooms on Allegheny serviceberry (*Amelanchier laevis*)

Plant name
Japanese maple (*Acer palmatum*)
Red maple (*Acer rubrum*)
Apple serviceberry (*Amelanchier grandiflora* cultivars)
Allegheny serviceberry (*Amelanchier laevis*)
Yellowwood (*Cladrastis lutea*)
Flowering dogwood (*Cornus florida*)
Kousa dogwood (*Cornus kousa*)
Washington hawthorn (*Crataegus phaenopyrum*)
Winter King hawthorn (*Crataegus viridis* 'Winter King')
Crape myrtle (*Lagerstroemia indica*)
Flowering crabapples (*Malus* cultivars)
Sourwood (*Oxydendrum arboreum*)
Sargent cherry (*Prunus sargentii*)
Japanese flowering cherry (*Prunus serrulata*)
Chinese quince (*Pseudocydonia sinensis*)
Callery pear (*Pyrus calleryana* 'Autumn Blaze', 'Redspire', or 'Chanticleer')
Sassafras (*Sassafras albidum*)
European mountain ash (*Sorbus aucuparia*)
Korean stewartia (*Stewartia pseudocamellia* 'Korean Beauty')

announce the early spring, giving way to red-orange autumn foliage and striped gray bark in winter. Flowering dogwood (*Cornus florida*) is truly a tree for four seasons, with showy spring flowers, shiny red summer fruit, crimson autumn foliage, and fissured, blocky winter bark. Korean stewartia (*Stewartia pseudocamellia* 'Korean Beauty'), bears flowers like single camellias in midsummer; its foliage turns gold to yellow-orange in autumn, and its multicolored bark peels off in large, spectacular, rounded flakes for interest all winter long.

Use the chart below to develop a landscape with seasonal drama throughout all the seasons of the year.

Spectacular spring flowers (facing page, left) and bright fall color (right) are only two of the seasonal effects for which flowering dogwood is noted. Add in attractive late-summer fruits and strong winter sculpture, and you have a true, 4-season all-star.

IN THIS CHAPTER

All-Star Trees **16**
Showy Flowers **18**
Showy Summer Foliage **20**
Showy Fall Foliage **21**
Late-Season Display **22**
Evergreens **24**

MULTISEASON ALL-STARS

Spring	Summer	Autumn	Winter
Attractive new foliage	Green summer foliage	Strong fall color	Sculptural winter form
Haze of red flowers	Good shade tree	Strong fall color	Good winter structure
White flowers	Attractive fruit	Strong fall color	Silvery bark
Bronze foliage, white flowers	Attractive fruit	Strong fall color	Good winter form
Attractive bark and foliage	Attractive white flowers	Strong fall color	Attractive structure
Spectacular flowers	Good foliage, red berries	Fall color	Horizontal winter structure
Spectacular flowers	Good foliage, red berries	Fall color	Good winter structure, bark
White flowers	Lustrous green leaves	Fall color	Showy fruit
White flowers	Lustrous green leaves	Fall color	Showy fruit and bark
	Spectacular flowers	Strong fall color	Showy bark and structure
Covered with flowers	Good foliage	Colorful fruit	Attractive structure
	White tassel-like flowers	Strong fall color, white fruits	Good winter structure
Pink flowers	Good foliage	Strong fall color	Very attractive bark
Attractive flowers	Good foliage	Occasional fall color	Attractive bark, structure
Pink flowers	Attractive fruit	Strong fall color	Attractive bark
Brilliant white flowers	Good foliage and form	Fall color	Distinctive structure
Yellow flowers before foliage	Good foliage	Neon fall color	
	White flowers	Bright, dramatic berries	Good structure
	Camellia-like flowers	Fall color	Outstanding bark

SHOWY FLOWERS

Everyone has a special place in their heart for flowering trees because of their spectacular blooms. For many trees, peak flowering is late spring and early summer, but some bloom from early spring until autumn. Yoshino cherries (*Prunus × yedoensis*), for example, flower briefly; watch quickly or you'll miss them. Stewartia, on the other hand, remains in bloom for more than a month. A few, like bottlebrush (*Callistemon*), flower most of the year in mild climates. Choose a tree for its size and shape, in addition to its flowers. Plant medium-height trees with wide canopies in front of taller, denser trees or next to buildings. If there is room, plant several to increase the effect.

Weeping Higan cherry (left) and goldenchain tree (above)

Pink flowering dogwood (above) and crabapple 'Profusion' (right)

Serviceberry (left) and white fringetree (above)

FLOWERING TIMES OF TREES

Tree	Spr. E	Spr. M	Spr. L	Sum. E	Sum. M	Sum. L	Fall
Red maple (*Acer rubrum*)	■						
Serviceberries (*Amelanchier* species)	■						
Bottlebrush (*Callistemon*)	■	■	■	■	■	■	■
Eastern redbud (*Cercis canadensis*)	■						
Sassafras (*Sassafras albidum*)	■						
Empress tree (*Paulownia tomentosa*)		■					
Cherry plum (*Prunus cerasifera* cultivars)		■					
Sargent cherry (*Prunus sargentii*)		■					
Japanese flowering cherries (*Prunus serrulata*)		■					
Callery pear (*Pyrus calleryana*)		■					
Flowering dogwood (*Cornus florida*)			■				
Saucer magnolia (*Magnolia × soulangiana*)		■					
Flowering crabapples (*Malus* species and cultivars)			■				
Carolina silverbell (*Halesia tetraptera*)			■				
Bigleaf magnolia (*Magnolia macrophylla*)				■			
Red horsechestnut (*Aesculus × carnea* 'Briotii')			■				
Horsechestnut (*Aesculus hippocastanum*)			■				
Yellowwood (*Cladrastis lutea*)				■			
Southern magnolia (*Magnolia grandiflora*)				■	■	■	

Japanese stewartia

Tree	Spr. E	Spr. M	Spr. L	Sum. E	Sum. M	Sum. L	Fall
White fringe tree (*Chionanthus virginicus*)			■				
Dove tree (*Davidia involucrata*)			■				
European mountain ash (*Sorbus aucuparia*)			■				
Hawthorns (*Craetagus*)			■				
Golden chain tree (*Laburnum* × *watereri*)			▪				
Black locust (*Robinia pseudoacacia*)			■				
Japanese snowbell (*Styrax japonicus*)			■				
Kousa dogwood (*Cornus kousa*)				■			
Japanese tree lilac (*Syringa reticulata*)			■				
Southern catalpa (*Catalpa bignonioides*)				■			
Silk tree or mimosa (*Albizia julibrissin*)				■			
Red-flowering gum (*Eucalyptus ficifolia*)					■		
Japanese stewartia (*Stewartia pseudocamellia*)					■		
Golden rain tree (*Koelreuteria paniculata*)					■		
Crape myrtle (*Lagerstroemia indica*)					■		
Five-stamen tamarisk (*Tamarix ramosissima*)					■		
Sourwood (*Oxydendrum arboreum*)					■		
Chaste tree (*Vitex agnus-castus*)					■		
Japanese pagoda tree (*Sophora japonica*)						■	
Franklin tree (*Franklinia alatamaha*)							■

Franklin tree (above)

Crape myrtle 'Seminole' (above)

Goldenrain tree (above)

Silk tree (above)

Red flowering gum (above)

Sourwood (right)

Southern magnolia (above)

Dove tree

Red horsechestnut

SHOWY SUMMER FOLIAGE

Many trees have cultivars selected for colorful foliage that rivals the beauty of flowers—and lasts all summer long. From somber, near-black purples and reds, through gentle hues of white, silver, and blue, to screaming pinks and yellows, trees with colorful foliage deserve careful consideration:; their long-term effect will be something you'll live with through many months each year. Most work best against a background of green. Use them sparingly—one red-leaved Japanese maple can go a long way; too many can be overbearing.

Tingirini gum

Flowering dogwood 'Welchii'

Black locust 'Frisia'

Giant dogwood 'Variegata'

Norway maple 'Royal Red'

European beech 'Punicea'

Colorado blue spruce

Boxelder maple 'Flamingo'

Kousa dogwood 'Wolfexe'

Sycamore maple 'Brilliantisimum'

Flowering dogwood 'First Lady'

SHOWY SUMMER FOLIAGE

Boxelder cultivars
  (*Acer negundo* 'Flamingo' and 'Variegatum')
Japanese maple cultivars
  (*Acer palmatum*)
Norway maple cultivars
  (*Acer platanoides* 'Crimson King' and 'Drummondii')

Eastern redbud
  (*Cercis canadensis* 'Forest Pansy')
European beech
  (*Fagus sylvatica* 'Purpurea', 'Riversii', 'Rohanii', 'Rosea-marginata', and 'Zlatia')

Sweet gum
  (*Liquidambar styraciflua* 'Burgundy' and 'Palo Alto'™)
Royalty flowering crabapple
  (*Malus* 'Royalty')

Purple-leaved cherry plums
  (*Prunus cerasifera* 'Newport' and 'Thundercloud')
Willow-leaved pear
  (*Pyrus salicifolia*)
Silver linden
  (*Tilia tomentosa*)

SHOWY FALL FOLIAGE

Brilliant autumn foliage lets even those trees that have gone unnoticed in the other seasons claim the spotlight. Some have one characteristic fall color; others display different colors all at once. Try to show them off against a good dark green background of evergreens. Fall color will vary: with the climate and soil, from season to season, and from tree to tree. To keep this variability to a minimum, try to buy your tree from the nursery in the fall when you can see its color. The accompanying list of trees with showy fall color includes a number of trees that are well known, but you'll find others that may surprise you. Use the list and the selection guide to help you select your own planting of fall show-offs.

Japanese maple

Japanese maple 'Osakazuki'

Larch

Sourwood

Red maple

Tulip tree

European beech

Ginkgo

OUTSTANDING AUTUMN FOLIAGE

Amur maple
  (*Acer ginnala*)
Japanese maple
  (*Acer palmatum*)
Red maple
  (*Acer rubrum*)
Sugar maple
  (*Acer saccharum*)
Apple serviceberry
  (*Amelanchier grandiflora*)
Allegheny serviceberry
  (*Amelanchier laevis*)
Pawpaw
  (*Asimina triloba*)
Paper birch
  (*Betula papyrifera*)
Katsura tree
  (*Cercidiphyllum japonicum*)
White fringe tree
  (*Chionanthus virginicus*)

Flowering dogwood
  (*Cornus florida*)
Kousa dogwood (*Cornus kousa*)
Cockspur hawthorn
  (*Crataegus crus-galli*)
Persimmon
  (*Diospyros*)
American beech
  (*Fagus grandiflora*)
Franklin tree
  (*Franklinia alatamaha*)
White ash
  (*Fraxinus americana*)
Green ash
  (*Fraxinus pennsylvanica*)
Ginkgo
  (*Ginkgo biloba*)
Crape myrtle
  (*Lagerstroemia indica*)
Sweet gum
  (*Liquidambar styraciflua*)

Tulip tree
  (*Liriodendron tulipifera*)
Black gum or tupelo
  (*Nyssa sylvatica*)
Sourwood
  (*Oxydendrum arboreum*)
Chinese pistachio
  (*Pistacia chinensis*)
Quaking aspen
  (*Populus tremuloides*)
Sargent cherry
  (*Prunus sargentii*)
Flowering cherry
  (*Prunus serrulata*)
Chinese quince
  (*Pseudocydonia sinensis*)
Golden larch
  (*Pseudolarix amabilis*)
Callery pear
  (*Pyrus calleryana cultivars*)
White oak
  (*Quercus alba*)

Scarlet oak
  (*Quercus coccinea*)
Chinese tallow tree
  (*Sapium sebiferum*)
Sassafras
  (*Sassafras albidum*)
European mountain ash
  (*Sorbus aucuparia*)
Japanese stewartia
  (*Stewartia pseudocamellia*)
Bald cypress
  (*Taxodium distichum*)
Littleleaf linden
  (*Tilia cordata*)
Elms
  (*Ulmus spp.*)
Japanese zelkova
  (*Zelkova serrata*)

LATE-SEASON DISPLAY

COLORFUL FRUIT

Fruit-bearing trees often keep their fruit longer than their flowers. Some are also "for the birds" and will help animate your garden with these feathered friends. Some fruit trees, such as serviceberry (*Amelanchier*), ripen by midsummer and become food for early birds. Others ripen in late summer, such as the flowering dogwood (*Cornus florida*). The fruit of American holly (*Ilex opaca*) and Washington hawthorn (*Crataegus phaenopyrum*) is not palatable until late winter (and waits for the birds of spring). Meanwhile, it adds a touch of color to the landscape.

Crabapple

Crabapple

Black gum, tupelo

Goldenrain tree

'Indian Magic' crabapple

European mountain ash

English holly

Sourwood

Kousa dogwood

TREES WITH SHOWY FRUIT

Amur maple
   (*Acer ginnala*)
Oriental persimmon (*Diospyros kaki*)
Flowering dogwood (*Cornus florida*)
Kousa dogwood
   (*Cornus kousa*)
Washington hawthorn (*Crataegus phaenopyrum*)
Winter King hawthorn (*Crataegus viridis* 'Winter King')

American holly
   (*Ilex opaca*)
Golden rain tree (*Koelreuteria paniculata*)
Flowering crabapples (*Malus* species and cultivars)
Magnolias
   (*Magnolia* spp.)
Black gum
   (*Nyssa sylvatica*)

Sourwood
   (*Oxydendrum arboreum*)
Chinese quince
   (*Pseudocydonia sinensis*)
Pepper tree
   (*Schinus molle*)
European mountain ash
   (*Sorbus aucuparia*)

DISTINCTIVE BARK

When was the last time you thought of a tree in terms of its bark? It's the most often-overlooked feature of a tree, but in some it's an outstanding asset. And it can add to the look of the tree year-round. Bark character, in fact, is the most interesting aspect of the paperbark maple (*Acer griseum*), paper birch (*Betula papyrifera*), and Amur chokecherry (*Prunus maackii*). It's an interest that is present all the time but more noticeable when the tree is without its leaves. There are evergreens, too, such as false cypress (*Chamaecyparis*), and redwood (*Sequoia sempervirens*) with striking bark interest. In these trees, the bark is an up-close feature, but it nevertheless adds to the appeal of the tree.

Mindaneo gum

Scotch pine

Paperbark maple

Japanese stewartia

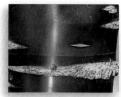
Lacebark pine

Paperbark cherry

Kousa dogwood

Paper birch

American beech

Chinese elm

River birch

Crape myrtle

TREES WITH SHOWY BARK

Paperbark maple
(*Acer griseum*)
River birch
(*Betula nigra*)
Paper birch
(*Betula papyrifera*)
Kousa dogwood
(*Cornus kousa*)
Eucalyptus
(*Eucalyptus* spp.)
Crape myrtle
(*Lagerstroemia indica*)
Amur cork tree
(*Phellodendron amurense*)
Lace-bark pine
(*Pinus bungeana*)

Plane tree, sycamore
(*Platanus* spp.)
Quaking aspen
(*Populus tremuloides*)
Amur chokecherry
(*Prunus maackii*)
Sargent cherry
(*Prunus sargentii*)
Chinese quince
(*Pseudocydonia sinensis*)
Japanese stewartia
(*Stewartia pseudocamellia*)
Chinese elm
(*Ulmus parvifolia*)

WINTER STRUCTURE

Winter is the time when the structure of trees comes into its own. No longer shrouded in a mantle of foliage or adorned with berries and flowers, the arching or upright limbs and branches are now what we see first. For certain trees, it's this framework that is their most outstanding feature, and it shows only after the leaves have fallen. Then, sculptural trees truly dominate the winter garden. Highlight, for example, the intricate weeping habit of a cutleaf Japanese maple or the twisting branches of a contorted Hankow willow by planting one near the front walk. Visitors will never fail to comment, winter or summer, about this unusual and unique tree.

Many other weeping trees are sculptural, but those with spreading branches are also outstanding in the winter. They may take a while to reach their peak but are well worth the wait.

TREES WITH SCULPTURAL WINTER FORM

Japanese maple
(*Acer palmatum*)
European hornbeam (*Carpinus betulus*)
American beech
(*Fagus grandifolia*)
Weeping European beech
(*Fagus sylvatica* 'Pendula')
Red Jade weeping crabapple
(*Malus* 'Red Jade')
Dawn redwood (*Metasequoia glyptostroboides*)
Amur cork tree
(*Phellodendron amurense*)
Tanyosho pine (*Pinus densiflora* 'Umbraculifera')

Saucer magnolia

Weeping cherry (*Prunus subhirtella* 'Pendula')
Corkscrew willow
(*Salix matsudana* 'Scarlet Curls' and 'Tortuosa')

EVERGREENS

Evergreens are useful and beautiful through the year. In the winter they offer strong green color and show off gracefully against snow. In spring, they provide the perfect counterpoint to flowering trees and intensify the effect of showy blooms. And any season of the year, they are the trees of choice for screening views and blocking wind and noise. Colorado blue spruce (left) and American arborvitae (above).

DECIDUOUS CONIFERS

European larch
(*Larix decidua*)

Japanese larch
(*Larix kaempferi*)

Dawn redwood
(*Metasequoia glyptostroboides*)

Golden larch
(*Pseudolarix amabilis*)

Bald cypress
(*Taxodium distichum*)

Looking for a permanent fixture in your landscape? Consider evergreens—their year-round interest can unify your garden through the seasons. Also, in winter they contrast with the stark outlines of deciduous trees and take on a whole different look because of this. Within this class of plants, there are needle and broadleaf evergreens; they vary both in the conditions they prefer and in their landscape uses.

NEEDLE EVERGREENS: Needle evergreens are called conifers because they bear cones. Most are pyramidal or conical, at least while young, and prefer full sun. Some, however, benefit from light shade, and a few, such as hemlocks (*Tsuga*) and yews (*Taxus*), will tolerate considerable shade. Most need little or no pruning if you give them growing space. Slower-growing conifers will save you time and effort (and space in small places).

BROADLEAF EVERGREENS: Broadleaved evergreens have leaves that overwinter. They lose their leaves, but unlike deciduous trees, only after a new set has appeared. Most prefer mild climates, and very few will survive northern winters. Some offer bright red berries in the winter, such as American and English hollies (*Ilex opaca* and *I. aquifolium*), while others have huge, waxy white flowers in spring and summer, such as southern magnolia (*Magnolia grandiflora*).

DECIDUOUS CONIFERS: Not all conifers hold their leaves in winter. A few lose their leaves in fall. They offer an interesting combination of leaves, cones, and tree shapes like needle evergreens with fall foliage color before they drop their leaves. And because they do lose their leaves, in the winter they bring unique silhouettes and trunk and branch shapes to the garden. They usually don't color as dramatically as deciduous trees, but instead offer a more muted color palette with which to experiment.

ODD-SHAPED EVERGREENS: Evergreens may be constant in their color, but they are not so in their shape—they come as tall pyramids and dwarf cones, and in conical, weeping, columnar, and open forms. One columnar 'Skyrocket' juniper will punctuate a flower bed; two can bring formality to an entryway. The Tanyosho pine, wide and spreading over its trunks, almost qualifies as a sculpture in the garden.

BROADLEAF EVERGREEN TREES

Lemon bottlebrush
  (*Callistemon
  citrinus*)
Camphor tree
  (*Cinnamomum
  camphora*)
Loquat
  (*Eriobotrya
  japonica*)

Eucalyptus or gum
  (*Eucalyptus* spp.)
American holly
  (*Ilex opaca*)
Southern magnolia
  (*Magnolia
  grandiflora*)
Olive
  (*Olea europaea*)

Cherry laurel
  (*Prunus
  laurocerasus*)
Coast live oak
  (*Quercus agrifolia*)
Pepper tree
  (*Schinus molle*)

EVERGREENS WITH COLORFUL FOLIAGE

Colorful evergreen foliage brightens your garden. Blue-toned conifers, such as blue Atlas cedar or Hoops blue spruce, mix well with other evergreens or bright flower colors. Yellow-tinged trees, such as golden chamaecyparis, work well as a focal point, or as a contrast with duller colors, such as gray or maroon-red.

NEEDLE EVERGREEN TREES

Firs (*Abies* spp.)
False cypresses
  (*Chamaecyparis* species)
Japanese cedar
  (*Cryptomeria japonica*)
Leyland cypress
  (*Cupressocyparis* × *leylandii*)
Monterey cypress
  (*Cupressus macrocarpa*)
Italian cypress
  (*Cupressus sempervirens*)
Spruces
  (*Picea* species)

Pines (*Pinus* species)
Yew pine
  (*Podocarpus macrophyllus*)
Japanese umbrella pine
  (*Sciadopitys verticillata*)
Redwood
  (*Sequoia sempervirens*)
Giant sequoia
  (*Sequoiadendron giganteum*)
American arborvitae
  (*Thuja occidentalis*)
Canada hemlock
  (*Tsuga canadensis*)

THE RIGHT TREE FOR THE PLACE

REGION AND ZONE

To find the best trees for your garden, you must know the right trees for your region. So before choosing your trees, arm yourself with information on your regional climate.

First, find out how cold it gets, on average, in your winters. Consult the map for your USDA hardiness zone (a division of the country by average minimum temperature). The hardiness of a tree (its ability to survive winter cold) will determine first if it's suited to your region.

Cold temperatures are one factor—high temperatures are another. Dallas and Seattle, for example, are both in zone 8 because their winter lows are similar. Their highs, however, are vastly different, and so are the kinds of trees that grow well in each city.

Consider also the amount of annual precipitation. It is more than 25 inches in most of the eastern half of the United States and less in most of the western half. Also, evaporation is so high in many areas that rainfall cannot keep up. Where this is the case, choose trees that can stand drought, or you'll be fighting a losing battle.

Trees native to river bottoms—red maple, sweet gum, pin oak, and bald cypress—are a special group. They tolerate the wet soil of their habitats but are surprisingly drought tolerant, too. Periodic flooding causes physiological drought, which reduces oxygen to the tree roots, a condition they adapt to.

These are the major factors, but others are explained here as well. Choose carefully, and your trees will thrive with very few problems.

GENERAL CLIMATIC REGIONS

Coastal Pacific Northwest: Mild winters and mild summers, along with moist conditions (except for two months in late summer) allow gardeners in this area to choose from a large list of native and exotic trees. Many conifers grow rapidly in the high humidity.

MEDITERRANEAN CALIFORNIA: The mild winters and warm, dry summers of the California coast are similar to the Mediterranean. Gardeners here also have a long list of native and exotic trees to work with.

SOUTHWEST: This region has extreme heat and aridity, but with irrigation, its list of useful trees is long. Currently, however, the emphasis is on drought-tolerant species and desert natives to deal with these conditions.

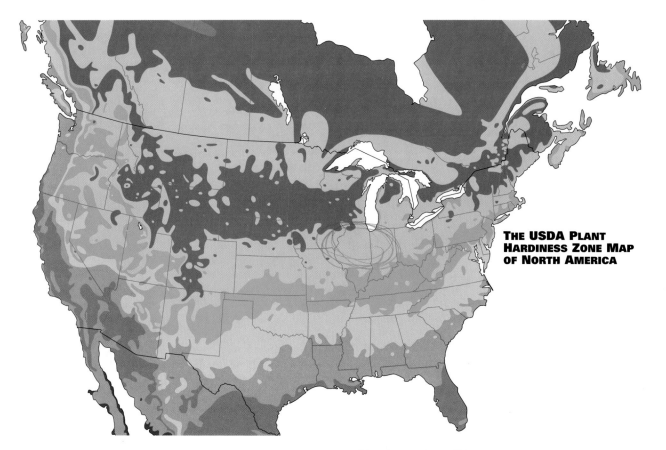

**THE USDA PLANT
HARDINESS ZONE MAP
OF NORTH AMERICA**

Range of Average Annual Minimum Temperatures for Each Zone

Zone 1: Below -50° F (below -45.6° C)
Zone 2: -50 to -40° F (-45.5 to -40° C)
Zone 3: -40 to -30° F (-39.9 to -34.5° C)
Zone 4: -30 to -20° F (-34.4 to -28.9° C)
Zone 5: -20 to -10° F (-28.8 to -23.4° C)
Zone 6: -10 to 0° F (-23.3 to -17.8° C)
Zone 7: 0 to 10° F (-17.7 to -12.3° C)
Zone 8: 10 to 20° F (-12.2 to -6.7° C)
Zone 9: 20 to 30° F (-6.6 to -1.2° C)
Zone 10: 30 to 40° F (-1.1 to 4.4° C)
Zone 11: Above 40° F (above 4.5° C)

IN THIS CHAPTER

Region and Zone **26**
Soil, Light and Air **28**
Analyzing Your Site **30**
Tree Habitats **31**
Small-Space Trees **32**

NORTHEAST AND APPALACHIANS: This humid region has cold winters and mild, humid summers and is well known for the colorful fall foliage of its native trees.

SOUTHEAST: This region is moist, with mild winters and long, hot summers. The geography within the region includes both swampy lowlands and drier hardwood forests.

MIDWEST AND PLAINS: This inland region has winters comparable to those of the Northeast but with colder temperatures, hotter summers, higher winds, and less moisture.

SOIL, LIGHT, AND AIR

When squeezed lightly, loam sticks together, but more pressure crumbles it.

After your regional climate, the condition of your soil is the next most important factor in the success of your trees. Soil (in addition to its organic matter) has three main ingredients—sand, silt, and clay—each made up of different-size particles, and each with very different physical properties as well.

SOIL

SOIL TYPES: Sand is coarse, silt is microscopic, and clay particles are so small they are visible only with an electron microscope. Sandy soils will fall apart in your hand. Silt soil will feel greasy, and clay soil will clump together. Loam, which is usually the best general soil type, is roughly an equal mixture of these three types plus organic matter (which is decomposing organic material such as leaf mold).

But apart from this combination, plants also need the correct density of soil to allow air and water circulation. Soils that are too sandy drain too quickly and starve the tree of moisture. Clay soils, on the other hand, stick together and choke the roots. Compacted soil has very poor circulation as well. Even good loose soil can become compacted by construction or carelessness on the part of the gardener. Even walking on wet soil can cause some compaction.

PH BALANCE: Before you plant, it will also help you to know something about soil pH. Soil pH is a measure of its relative acidity or alkalinity, measured on a 14-point scale. Midway, 7 is considered neutral; lower numbers are acidic, higher numbers, alkaline. It's an important measure because pH extremes interfere with the ability of a tree to absorb nutrients. Most trees grow well in soils with a pH of 4.5 to 6.5, (slightly acidic) but many will tolerate wider ranges. You can test your soil pH with a simple kit purchased at your garden center. For a complete analysis, contact your local extension office.

Soil added to water and allowed to sit will settle into layers of water, silt, and clay, giving you a rough idea of your soil type.

NUTRIENTS: There are three primary nutrients (nitrogen, phosphorus, and potassium) and numerous secondary nutrients necessary for tree growth. Nitrogen fosters foliage growth and color, phosphorous promotes root development, and potassium is necessary for general health. Other elements, such as calcium, magnesium, iron, and sulfur, are just as vital, but are needed in smaller amounts. Tree roots take these nutrients from the soil, and most soils already have adequate amounts.

TREES FOR DRY, SANDY SOILS

Amur maple
  (*Acer ginnala*)
Boxelder
  (*Acer negundo*)
Ohio buckeye
  (*Aesculus glabra*)
Hackberry
  (*Celtis occidentalis*)
Russian olive
  (*Elaeagnus angustifolia*)
Green ash
  (*Fraxinus pennsylvanica*)
Thornless honey locust
  (*Gleditsia triacanthos* var. *inermis* cultivars)
Eastern red cedar
  (*Juniperus virginiana*)
Black locust
  (*Robinia pseudoacacia*)
Chinese tallow tree
  (*Sapium sebiferum*)

TREES THAT TOLERATE WET SOILS

Red maple
  (*Acer rubrum*)
Silver maple
  (*Acer saccharinum*)
Alder
  (*Alnus* spp.)
River birch
  (*Betula nigra*)

Sweet gum
  (*Liquidambar styraciflua*)
Black gum
  (*Nyssa sylvatica*)
Plane tree (*Platanus* spp.)
Willow (*Salix* spp.)
Bald cypress
  (*Taxodium distichum*)

POLLUTION-TOLERANT TREES

European hornbeam
  (*Carpinus betulus*)
Hackberry
  (*Celtis*)
Fringe tree
  (*Chionanthus*)
Hawthorn
  (*Crataegus*)
Honey locust
  (*Gleditsia*)
Plane tree
  (*Platanus*)
Japanese pagoda tree
  (*Sophora japonica*)

LIGHT

Choosing the best location for your trees will involve taking an inventory of the sun and shade patterns in your landscape—and they're different at different times of the day and year. In late June, the sun rises northeast, is high overhead at noon, and sets in the northwest sky. In late March and September, it rises in the east, sets west, and is lower at noon. By late December, its course is a low arc in the southern sky. The greatest heat strikes western walls and windows in early summer but south walls and windows in winter. For summer shade, plant trees on the west and keep the south side open to the winter sun. A discussion of siting and microclimates follows on pages 30 and 31.

AIR

Often overlooked, air circulation is crucial to healthy growth. Without it, humidity favors disease-causing fungi. Give your trees enough space; plant disease-prone trees in breezy sites, (or better yet, plant disease-resistant trees), and rake up infected leaves as they fall.

Air pollution can also limit tree growth. Tree leaves will absorb some pollution, but they can be damaged where levels of pollutants are heavy and constant, in highway locations for example.

TREES TOLERANT OF SHADE

Japanese maple
(*Acer palmatum*)
Allegheny serviceberry
(*Amelanchier laevis*)
Eastern redbud
(*Cercis canadensis*)
White fringe tree
(*Chionanthus virginicus*)
Flowering dogwood
(*Cornus florida*)
Kousa dogwood
(*Cornus kousa*)
American holly
(*Ilex opaca*)
Carolina silverbell
(*Halesia tetraptera*)
Bigleaf magnolia
(*Magnolia macrophylla*)
Sourwood
(*Oxydendrum arboreum*)
Canadian hemlock
(*Tsuga canadensis*)

CHANGING SHADE PATTERNS THROUGH THE YEAR

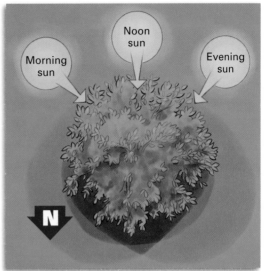

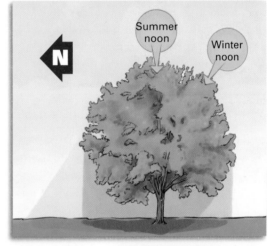

Certain trees such as this bigleaf magnolia, are shade tolerant and will happily grow in the high shade of taller trees. This magnolia also benefits from the wind protection given by such a site.

ANALYZING YOUR SITE

Before planting something as permanent as a tree, look at your property as a whole to determine its planting assets and liabilities. Make a rough sketch; show the house, sidewalks, and other features that will affect your overall plan. Make note of the terrain; then decide which existing trees and shrubs to keep. If your site is wooded, for example, you may want to remove trees to make room for more desirable varieties or to let more sunlight fall on the property.

Note north and south on your sketch. South- and west-facing walls receive more sun, north- and east-facing walls receive less. Plant trees south and west of an area to shade it. (Remember that deciduous trees will offer shade in the summer but let the winter sun in.) Note low spots that collect rainwater.

Trees planted in these areas need to be tolerant of wet soil. Consider also the direction of prevailing winter winds; deflect them with an evergreen windbreak. And don't overlook the view from indoors. Plant flowering or sculptural trees where they can be seen from inside. Screen objectionable views with taller, denser trees.

Finally, consider unique features that you want to highlight—a garden shed, a natural rock outcrop, or a small hill. Weeping cherry can serve as a beautiful backdrop for a garden shed or other small building. Plant a picturesque evergreen near an outcrop or a group of redbuds on a small rise. Also, before you finalize your plan, make sure you haven't created traffic problems for vehicles or for foot traffic.

MICROCLIMATES IN YOUR GARDEN

As you analyze your property, you will notice different microclimates in your landscape. These are small areas where climate and soil conditions can vary widely from the average (and from each other). There may be a spot rain never reaches under a roof overhang. Another area may heat up quickly in the morning. A narrow space between the house and garage might be a small-scale wind tunnel. Take advantage of these microclimates by planting trees suited to them. South-facing walls or inside corners will trap heat; that's the spot for spring-flowering trees like the Kousa dogwood. But a star magnolia, which already flowers very early, might be more vulnerable to late spring frosts in that heat trap, so plant it in a cooler, shady area, where it will flower after the chance of freezing is past.

1. North-facing slope
2. High, bright shade (honey locust)
3. Exposed top of hill
4. South-facing slope—rock outcrop
5. Dense shade (maple)
6. Low wet spot (frost pocket)
7. Dense shade (hemlock)
8. North-facing walls under overhang
9. East-facing wall
10. Western exposure (hot)
11. South-facing brick wall (hot)

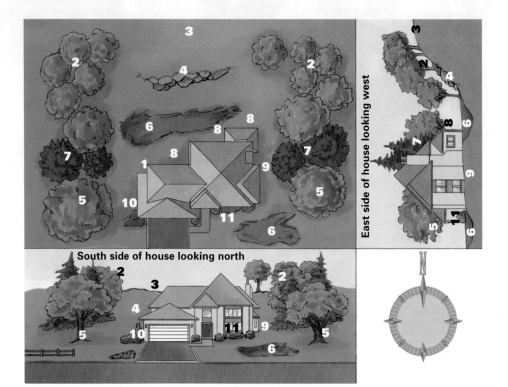

TREE HABITATS

In choosing trees that will succeed, you'll want to make the best match between the adaptability of the tree and the conditions in which you'll plant it. As you ponder your choices, you may want to consider naturally occurring habitats. These bring climatic and soil conditions together in specific ways and can offer clues to what kind of trees might thrive in similar conditions in your landscape.

In nature, trees which withstand periodic drought and flood are well suited to the neglect, air pollution, reflected heat, compacted soils, and limited root space that street trees must endure.

TREES ADAPTED TO SPECIFIC HABITATS

WOODLANDS: Moist woodlands are home to maples (*Acer*), hornbeams (*Carpinus*), beeches (*Fagus*), and others that do best in well-drained soil with reliable moisture and nutrients. Dry woodlands, on the other hand, are home to most hickories (*Carya*), eastern redbud (*Cercis canadensis*), many oaks (*Quercus*), and others that tolerate drier soils. Some make good street trees.

FLOOD PLAINS: River-bottom trees adapt to soils with imperfect drainage. You'll find red and silver maple (*Acer rubrum* and *A. saccharinum*), river birch (*Betula nigra*), sweet gum (*Liquidambar*), and others. Many of these are also successful as street trees because they are adapted to drought as well as flooding.

STONY OUTCROPS AND SLOPES: Thin, stony soils drain quickly and are very dry—perfect for most hawthorns (*Crataegus*), eastern red cedar (*Juniperus virginiana*), Chinese pistachio (*Pistacia chinensis*), black locust (*Robinia pseudoacacia*), and others that do well in dry sites.

FOREST EDGES: Woodland edges offer shade and wind protection and are home to eastern redbud (*Cercis canadensis*), flowering dogwood (*Cornus florida*), Carolina silverbell (*Halesia tetraptera*), and many others that grow well in these more protected conditions.

SEASHORE: Trees growing near salt water must withstand seaside salt spray, drought, and harsh winds. Camphor tree (*Cinnamomum camphora*), cypresses (*Cupressus*), eastern red cedar (*Juniperus virginiana*), and Japanese black pine (*Pinus thunbergii*) are among the best adapted here.

GOOD SEASHORE TREES

False cypress
  (*Chamaecyparis*)
Camphor tree
  (*Cinnamomum camphora*)
Cypress
  (*Cupressus*)
American holly (*Ilex opaca*)
Eastern red cedar
  (*Juniperus virginiana*)
Sweet bay
  (*Magnolia virginiana*)
Black gum
  (*Nyssa sylvatica*)
Japanese black pine
  (*Pinus thunbergii*)
Plane tree (*Platanus*)

Only the most rugged trees can withstand the rigors of the seashore. Monterey cypress is famous for its drama in seaside settings on the West Coast.

GOOD STREET TREES

Red maple (*Acer rubrum*)
Nonfruiting green ash
  (*Fraxinus pennsylvanica*
  'Marshall's Seedless')
Nonfruiting honey locust
  (*Gleditsia* cultivars)
Sargent cherry (*Prunus sargentii*)
Callery pear (*Pyrus calleryana* cultivars)

Willow oak
  (*Quercus phellos*)
Red oak (*Quercus rubra*)
Japanese pagoda tree
  (*Sophora japonica* cultivars)
Redmond linden
  (*Tilia americana* 'Redmond')
Japanese zelkova
  (*Zelkova serrata* 'Green Vase')

SMALL-SPACE TREES

Trees that are too tall and too wide are common along urban and suburban streets. They cause problems. But tall trees under utility lines cause serious problems. They will eventually have to be pruned to keep the lines clear, and drastic pruning creates an avenue of one-sided or topless trees. Smaller trees are available which fit neatly under overhead lines.

The number of trees suited to planting in a small space is actually quite large, and many of them will even fit into the most modest of sideyards, as shown here.

TREE ROOTS

No discussion about trees and space would be complete without a warning about tree roots. Trees with aggressive or invasive roots can crack sidewalks and roads, or attack sewage or drainage lines. If tree roots are cracking your sidewalk, just remove the tree completely. Do not plant trees with invasive roots, like silver maple (Acer saccharinum), willow (*Salix*), poplar (*Populus*), alder (Alnus), pepper tree (Schinus), and sweet gum (Liquidambar) near sewer lines, septic fields, wells, drainage lines, or sidewalks, streets and other paved areas. Their roots will seek out and clog the area or damage the lines, or grow under and damage the paving.

TREES FOR SMALL SPACES

Amur maple
  (Acer ginnala)
Globe Norway maple
  (Acer platanoides
  'Globosum')
Lemon bottlebrush
  (Callistemon citrinus)
American hornbeam
  (Carpinus caroliniana)
Eastern redbud
  (Cercis canadensis)
Carolina silverbell
  (Halesia tetraptera)
Golden rain tree
  (Koelreuteria paniculata)

Golden chain tree
  (Laburnum watereri)
Flowering crabapple
  (Malus 'Adirondack',
  'Beverly', 'David', other
  cultivars under 20 feet)
Amanogawa cherry
  (Prunus 'Amanogawa')
Okame cherry
  (Prunus 'Okame')
Kwanzan cherry
  (Prunus 'Sekiyama')
Japanese tree lilac
  (Syringa reticulata
  'Ivory Silk')

Plan your views carefully before planting a courtyard—consider the look from both indoors and outdoors.

TREES FOR SMALL LOTS

Plan carefully when you choose a tree for a small yard. Small spaces can be taken in at a glance, and whatever trees you plant will stand out immediately. They will almost always become a focal point.

With a limited space you need the hardest-working trees you can get, and many of the all-stars we introduced earlier do well in small spots. The Red Jade crabapple (*Malus* 'Red Jade'), with its long-lasting, bright fruit, and the small paperbark maple (*Acer griseum*), with its unique winter bark, give lots of interest late into the year. The graceful forms of Japanese maple (*Acer palmatum*) or flowering dogwood (*Cornus florida*) never lose their appeal. Just remember, keep all the seasons in mind when picking the tree for your lot.

CONTAINER TREES

When you're faced with very limited garden space and yet you still yearn to have some trees, you might think you have no options. But one alternative is to grow your small trees in containers.

The best trees to plant in containers are going to be naturally small to begin with. Also, another factor to consider is the shape of the tree. You don't want to try a tree that will be too top heavy in a container. Good shapes to try are conical or pyramidal, vase-shaped, shrubby, and columnar.

Once you pick out your tree, invest in the heaviest container you can afford so the tree won't blow over if caught in the wind. One advantage to growing trees in containers is that you have complete control over the placement of the tree. If you want to move it to a more visible spot when it's in bloom, you can. (Although be sure to fit the container with casters; moving even a small tree in a pot can be a real job sometimes.)

Another consideration when you're choosing a tree is the hardiness of the tree. Generally, because the container is exposed to the air instead of being insulated in the ground, you lose at least one zone of hardiness. That is, if the tree is normally hardy to zone 6, treat it as if it were hardy to zone 5 instead.

Both deciduous and evergreen trees can be planted successfully in containers, as in this rooftop garden.

TREE LITTER

One major consideration when choosing a tree is the amount of litter it might throw. If the site you've chosen doesn't need to be tidy and you have plenty of space, then it's not a worry. But for most people this is not the case, especially with trees hanging over paving.

Generally, tree litter means dropped flowers, seed capsules, fruit, or even excessive leaf drop. What this means for the homeowner unlucky enough to have such a tree near the street or a walkway is that he or she will either be constantly sweeping this up or else letting it pile up unattractively, and neither is a good option. By knowing ahead of time the habits of your potential tree, you can avoid a lot of work in the future.

The flowers of saucer magnolia can make a slippery mess when they start dropping. Avoid planting this tree over paved areas.

LITTER-PRONE TREES TO AVOID AROUND PAVING

Ash	Elm	Maple (for seeds)	Pepper tree
Black gum	Eucalyptus	Mimosa	Persimmon
Black walnut	Honey locust	Oak (for acorns)	Southern catalpa
Cherry plum	Female ginkgos	Olive	Sweet gum
Crabapple	Magnolia (for flowers)	Pecan	

PLANTING AND CARE

ACQUIRING TREES

The many sources of trees each have their own pluses and minuses. You can buy trees at a nursery or garden center or through a mail-order catalog (see our list of mail-order sources on page 93). A nursery usually grows some of its own stock and sells directly to the public. A garden center is a retail store, selling trees from wholesalers. At both sources you can see what you're buying and you can ask questions face to face. (Mail-order houses may have a larger selection, however.) If you are planning to buy a large tree, a nearby nursery or garden center is your best bet.

It's best to start with a healthy, well-formed, and relatively small tree. Small trees withstand transplant shock better and recover faster. In transplant shock, the root system cannot take in water fast enough to supply the top of the tree, and it may look wilted or sick. Lessen the shock by planting the tree on a cool, moist day and watering it in promptly. Late autumn and early spring are generally the best times to plant trees.

Balled-and-burlapped trees, their trunks wrapped for protection, are a common sight at nurseries everywhere. Getting them home safe and sound and in good health is the real trick.

HOW TREES ARE SOLD

Trees come bare root, (wrapped but with no soil around the roots), balled and burlapped, (with a ball of soil and roots wrapped in burlap), or in containers (large metal or compressed-fiber pots). Bare-root and balled-and-burlapped trees will have lost many of their feeding roots when dug from their home soil, and that loss can contribute to transplant shock. Container-grown trees will not have lost roots, but if they were recently transplanted from a smaller to larger container, they may still be in shock. Smaller trees come in all three kinds of packaging, but larger trees are normally balled and burlapped and sold in wire baskets. Which is best? That depends on the size of the tree, the time of year, and availability.

Container-grown trees are more tolerant of planting later in the season, when it is too late to plant balled-and-burlapped trees.

Normally, only smaller trees are sold bare root. Bare-root planting is best done in spring when the trees are fully dormant. Open the package and add moisture if the roots feel dry. Plant them soon—the same day, if possible, but in the meantime, keep them in a cool place, out of the sun. Two to four hours before planting, soak them in lukewarm water to help them store water for their move.

Most trees are sold balled and burlapped, and many are sold locally and are freshly dug from the ground. Like bare-root trees, they have already lost roots, so plant them as soon as you can. Until then, keep them in the shade. They'll be fine for a few weeks if you keep the rootballs moist, but never allow them to sit in water.

Container-grown trees are probably the most common form in which trees are sold. They are grown in a formulated soil mix, with slow-acting fertilizer, so they can be transplanted at almost any time of year. You'll have best results, however, if you plant in cool weather. Handle and store trees recently dug and placed in containers like balled-and-burlapped trees.

TRANSPORTING YOUR TREE

Trees can be brought home in any closed vehicle large enough for the whole tree or securely covered with a tarp in an open truck. The wind generated by highway speeds dries plants out rapidly, and it is hard for a tree that has dried in transit to recover. Wrap a few layers of burlap or similar material around the top to prevent wind burn, and around the trunk to prevent mechanical damage to the bark.

If you don't take steps to protect your new tree on the way home, your investment may be ruined. Securely wrapping the tree helps reduce the amount of dehydration the wind causes as well as physically protects the leaves from shredding or tattering.

IN THIS CHAPTER

Acquiring Trees **34**
Planting New Trees **36**
After Planting **38**
Caring for a
New Tree **39**
Pruning **40**
Caring for
Established Trees **42**

PLANTING NEW TREES

The successful tree needs not only the right site but also a healthy place for its roots. Roots grow outward and branch through the soil, absorbing water and nutrients. The reach of the root spread is usually well beyond that of its branches. New root growth is horizontal—in the top foot or two of soil. Roots need oxygen from the air, water and nutrients from the soil, and moderate temperatures.

Plant a bare-root tree so its roots are fanned out over a mound of soil and the tree is positioned at the nursery planting depth.

BARE-ROOT

First, carefully prune roots of all broken, damaged, and straggling tips. Dig the planting hole wide enough to accommodate the spread of the roots. Make a mound of soil in the center of the hole to support the trunk at its nursery depth, and spread the roots out over it. Fill the hole halfway with soil and then water to settle it. After this, fill the hole completely and water again. Do not compact the soil by stepping on it; you'll reduce the air space available to the roots.

BALLED AND BURLAPPED

Dig the hole four times as wide as the rootball but slightly less than its depth to minimize

With natural-burlap-wrapped trees, you first place the tree at the correct level, roll back the excess and trim it off, and then very gently firm the soil down, taking extra care not to compact the soil.

A PRUNING CAUTION

Past advice has held that you should prune the top of a tree when planting it, to reduce water stress to the new roots caused by competition from the top growth. Recent studies, however, have shown that this can be counter-productive for trees whose leaves have already appeared—the leaves are needed to make food for root growth. However, if you're moving a tree with a very small root system (which is not recommended), lightly thinning the top may be necessary for the survival of its roots.

settling. Loosening this large an area lets the roots spread to anchor the tree.

If your tree is balled and burlapped, determine whether the burlap is natural, preservative-treated (usually green), or plasticized. Remove preservative-treated or plasticized burlap and any rope or twine. If the ball is wrapped with natural burlap, set it in the hole, cut and roll back the burlap from the top, removing the excess. If the rootball is in a wire basket, remove it before planting.

SOIL AMENDMENTS

Recent studies have shown that most trees establish themselves faster when no soil amendments are added at planting. A soil heavily amended with peat moss, fertilizer, or formulated soil mix becomes overly moist and fertile. Roots will tend to remain in this pocket instead of growing outward into the surrounding soil to anchor the tree.

There are, however, two exceptions. First, when the soil texture and drainage of the rootball differs markedly from that of its new surroundings, the planting hole may need amendments. A clay rootball planted in sandy soil, for example, can act as an oasis and keep the roots within its boundaries. On the other hand, a sandy rootball planted in slow-draining clay may become waterlogged and rot. In either situation, amend the soil in the planting hole with compost, peat moss, or well-rotted manure.

Second, because phosphates don't travel far when added later and watered in, it's a good idea to add superphosphate or bone-meal to the bottom half of the backfill.

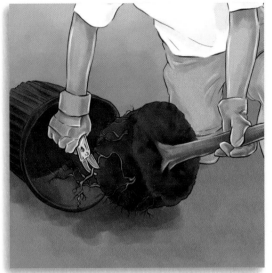

If a container tree has developed large, circling roots, they can be thinned lightly before planting, but this is not normally done.

CONTAINER-GROWN TREES

First, dig a hole the same size as you would for a balled and burlapped tree. Then remove the tree and loosen any roots that encircle the rootball, or cut vertically (about a third of the way up from the bottom) through outer roots at three places around the ball.

Hold the tree by the rootball (not by its trunk) and lower it into the planting hole. Be sure the rootball top is no lower than the ground line after settling. If you plant too deeply, you'll prevent the roots from getting adequate oxygen and hamper their water and nutrient absorption.

FINAL STEPS

With the rootball at its final depth, score it lightly on the sides to encourage roots to grow out into the new soil. Fill the hole halfway with unamended soil (see sidebar on page 36), and water gently to settle it. If your soil is low in phosphate, this is the time to stimulate root growth; mix a handful of superphosphate or bonemeal into the bottom half of the backfill. Fill the hole completely and form a ridge of soil around the edge to retain water. Fill this basin with water, let it drain, and fill it again. Check the soil moisture periodically at a 2- to 3-inch depth, and water before it becomes dry. Do not water clay soils as often as sandy soils because they drain more slowly.

By watering a newly planted tree thoroughly, you help settle the soil as well as lessen transplant shock. Make a mound of soil around the planting hole to help retain the water and mulch.

WHEN TO PLANT AND TRANSPLANT

In most parts of the country, early spring (while deciduous plants are still dormant and leafless) is the best time to plant any deciduous tree, and the only time you should plant bare-root trees. Leafless trees draw less water and nutrients from the roots, and recover more easily from transplant shock. For the same reason, balled-and-burlapped trees should be dug from the nursery when they're dormant in early spring, late fall, or even winter (if the ground isn't frozen). They can usually be held in the nursery longer than bare-root trees, and planted later in the spring or early summer with reasonable success. Container-grown trees, however, can be planted successfully nearly any time of the year, although cool, moist days are always best.

Planting in fall or winter is recommended in areas where summers are extreme and winters mild, such as the South (where summers are very hot) and the West (where summers are dry).

Trees with active late winter sap flow, such as birch and sugar maple, are risky choices for early spring transplanting. Wait until the sap flow ends, just as the leaf buds begin to unfold.

For spring planting of fleshy-rooted trees such as magnolias, it is best to wait until the leaves have expanded slightly.

Evergreens are best planted in early autumn, after summer heat is gone but early enough for full establishment.

Finally, remember that when planting or transplanting any tree, avoid hot, dry days.

AFTER PLANTING

Young trees with tender bark can benefit from trunk wrapping because it helps prevent sunscald and dehydration, as well as evening out temperature fluctuations. When wrapping trunks, be sure to start at the bottom and work your way up the trunk.

Now that your trees are safely planted, there are a few steps to take to provide them with further care.

TRUNK WRAPPING

Tree wrap is a crepe strip that insulates the bark against temperature fluctuations in late winter and prevents dehydration and trunk scald. It may not be necessary for some trees but is especially good for young, thin-barked varieties (a few maples, green ash, honey locust, golden chain tree, and cherries) the first winter after planting. Tree wrap can harbor insects and diseases; be sure to remove it in the spring.

STAKING

Staking a tree is root reinforcement—it keeps the tree from falling over or leaning until its roots are strong enough to anchor it. Most trees do not need staking, but bare-root trees, large evergreens, and top-heavy trees do. Make your staking loose enough to allow the trunk to flex both along its length and at its base.

The tree will respond by developing added strength in the trunk and anchor roots. Remove the stakes after one or two growing seasons, and the tree will develop faster.

STAKING DECIDUOUS TREES

Don't use the materials that were once standard—wire and garden hose. The hose constricts trunk growth. Instead, use 3-inch webbing or polyethylene strips twisted loosely at their midpoint once around the tree and attached to the stake with staples. Keep the strip as low as possible to allow the trunk to sway. Swaying is an exercise that promotes strong growth. Any tree with a trunk 3 inches or less in diameter needs only one stake, placed on the windward side, but you can use more for added stability. Larger trees should be staked in two or three directions.

STAKING EVERGREENS

Evergreens with branches close to the ground may not need staking, but tall trees or those in windy sites will. Evergreens are normally staked with three guy wires attached to the trunk at the same point with webbing or polyethylene strips. The guy wires radiate in equal angles from the trunk and down to anchor stakes, which should be driven into the ground parallel to the wires. In high-traffic areas (or where children play), use tall stakes and straps instead of guy wires.

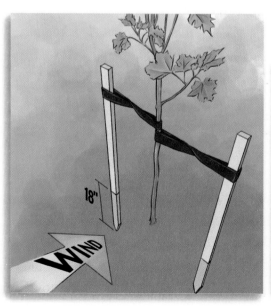

CARING FOR A NEW TREE

WATERING

During the first year after planting, water is the most important factor in new-tree nutrition. Deep, thorough watering done occasionally is much better than the constant shallow watering offered by sprinkling systems. Place a hose at the base of the tree and allow a trickle of water to flow for at least 15 minutes. Trees in sandy soils should be watered more often than trees in heavy soils. Heavy soils drain slowly, and you must allow time to elapse between waterings.

FERTILIZING

Fertilizing newly planted trees is not usually recommended. Most landscape soils have enough nutrients for trees, and a young nursery-grown tree itself is a storehouse of mineral nutrients. It is not likely that such a tree would become nutrient-deficient while establishing itself.

MULCHING

After planting and watering a tree, apply a 2- to 3-inch layer of mulch (never more than 4 inches) over the entire planting area. Organic mulches, such as shredded bark, conserve moisture and reduce the need for water by slowing down its evaporation from the surface. Their insulating properties help maintain more uniform soil temperatures, and that improves root growth and benefits bacteria, fungi, earthworms, and other organisms that keep the soil alive. Mulches also retard weed growth, create an attractive surface, and when used around trees, prevent lawn-mower damage to the trunks.

TYPES OF MULCH

Mulches are classified as organic or inorganic. Organic mulches include shredded bark, bark nuggets, wood chips, pine needles, and even composted leaves. Inorganic mulches are usually pea gravel or coarser aggregate. Shredded bark is a good choice because it binds together to make a loose mat and is not likely to float away in heavy rain. Avoid peat moss and fresh wood chips. The one blows away in the wind and can even catch fire, and the other steals nitrogen from the soil.

Shredded pine bark mulch

Pine bark mulch

Red cedar mulch

PROTECTING YOUNG TREES FROM ANIMAL DAMAGE

Deer and rabbits like young trees as much as the gardeners who planted them. They can easily bite off branches or chew bark completely off the trunk. Fortunately, there are steps you can take to prevent this. Protect young trees by enclosing them with chicken wire or wire mesh. Trunks of older trees can be protected from rodents and rabbits by ordinary tree wrap, but new flexible plastic tree protectors, available in a variety of lengths, loosely surround the tree trunk and are better.

PRUNING

Correct cut: at a 45-degree angle and ¼ inch above bud.

This cut is too far above the bud.

The angle of this cut is too steep.

This cut angles in the wrong direction.

This cut is too close to the bud.

Pruning can be used to remove diseased, damaged, or dead branches, to improve structure, and to increase vigor. It can mean trimming back branches or removing entire limbs. It can increase the yield of fruit and flowers and improve the health of a tree. But no matter what the reason, always have a plan. Improper pruning is worse than none.

THE PROPER CUT: Prune small branches about ¼ inch above an outward-facing bud to direct new growth away from the interior canopy. If you remove a large branch, make three cuts to avoid tearing the bark.

STRUCTURE: For the first five years, prune only to develop the framework of the tree. Select the strongest central upright branch as the "leader" and prune back competitors. Keep well-spaced lateral branches that give the tree a balanced look.

PRUNING CONIFERS: Most conifers do not tolerate pruning. Hemlocks and yew are exceptions, and pines may be pruned to make them denser by cutting back "candles" of new growth while they are soft.

MAINTENANCE: Certain pruning chores come up again and again, and it pays to know them and watch for them. Water sprouts (thin growth growing vertically from limbs) and suckers (thin growth arising around the base of the trunk) are two common things to look for and prune. Always watch for dead or diseased branches and remove them promptly. Branches growing toward the trunk or inward should be pruned as well. Also, branches with shallow crotch angles are weak and prone to breaking in high winds or storms; they should be removed.

And, if you'd like, you can always remove small branches purely to clean up the structure of the tree, to make it look better. Just remember to do this in moderation.

A wider crotch angle (left) is strong, while a narrower angle (right) is weak and prone to breaking.

PRUNING TOOLS

A pair of pruning shears is the tool you will use most. Scissor pruners cut cleaner than anvil shears. Anvil shears have a tendency to crush rather than cut neatly. And, because a pair of shears is such an important tool, invest in the best you can afford. It will pay dividends for years. With this handy tool and a folding saw, you'll be ready to handle most of your elementary pruning chores.

Later, you should also add lopping shears (for taking off branches surrounded by thick brush, such as small, interior limbs), a wide-blade pruning saw (for sawing larger branches), and an extension pole pruning saw (for cutting high branches).

SEVEN REASONS TO PRUNE

Keeping in mind the seven major reasons to prune helps to simplify the process and keep your efforts focused. Approach each tree in the following order:

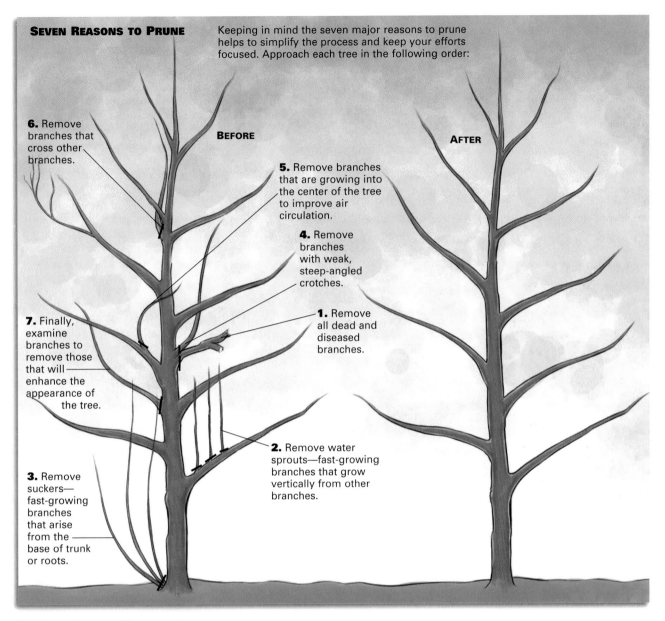

BEFORE

AFTER

6. Remove branches that cross other branches.

5. Remove branches that are growing into the center of the tree to improve air circulation.

4. Remove branches with weak, steep-angled crotches.

1. Remove all dead and diseased branches.

7. Finally, examine branches to remove those that will enhance the appearance of the tree.

2. Remove water sprouts—fast-growing branches that grow vertically from other branches.

3. Remove suckers— fast-growing branches that arise from the base of trunk or roots.

PRUNING LARGER BRANCHES

The first cut keeps the bark from tearing when the branch comes off.

The second cut removes the bulk of the branch.

The last cut removes the stub of the branch back to the collar.

Cutting too flush (top) or too far out (bottom) invites disease.

CARING FOR ESTABLISHED TREES

Established trees, such as this ancient katsura tree (Cercidiphyllum japonicum) are valuable investments to protect with care. One of the most important things you can do is avoid allowing lawn to grow up to the trunk. Use a mulched area underneath, instead.

PREVENTING CONSTRUCTION DAMAGE

You can protect trees in a construction site by following the guidelines offered in *Tree City, USA* Bulletin No. 20 of the National Arbor Day Foundation:

1. Before construction begins, remove all trees that are not to be saved.
2. Prune low-growing limbs that may be in the way of machinery.
3. Fertilize, water, and aerate trees that will be saved.
4. Install plastic mesh fences under the drip line.
5. Install siltation fences to keep soil from construction areas away from root zones.
6. Do not store materials within fenced-in areas.

A siltation fence protects a tree's root zone from soil buildup during construction.

Established trees do need some attention. They are not only less stress tolerant than younger trees, but are also worth more. Established trees can add 14 to 27 percent to the value of your home, and large, mature trees are especially valuable. Watering, pruning, mulching, and root-system care can improve their mature health.

FERTILIZING established healthy trees is normally not necessary. Do not fertilize "just to be safe." Unneeded fertilizer can promote succulent new growth vulnerable to pests.

Trees with deadwood or those that exhibit declining growth, leaf size, and color are candidates for fertilization and should be fertilized in early autumn or early spring. Use a broadcast lawn fertilizer over the root zone, at the same time you fertilize your lawn. Injection fertilizing is usually unnecessary.

WATERING DURING DROUGHT can help your tree, but water deeply or not at all. Add water to the root zone until at least the top 6 inches is moist (it may take longer than you expect). Then wait at least a week before watering again unless your soil is sandy.

PRUNING established trees is more a matter of maintenance than anything else. If the tree was trained properly while young, the leader and main scaffold branches should be growing correctly. But you need to watch the tree for dead, weak, diseased, broken or insect-infested branches and remove these promptly. Also remove low or crossing limbs. If anything more extensive than this seems necessary, an arborist should be consulted.

MULCHING established trees will result in better root activity and faster growth. It will also keep lawn mowers from damaging tree trunks (since you won't be mowing the mulch). Remove the turf (roots and all, with a spade or sod cutter) before you mulch and be sure not to pile mulch up against the trunk—it can make a home for insects and disease organisms.

ROOT-GROWTH PROMOTERS are preparations of mycorrhizal fungi that enhance tree root growth naturally. These organisms may already be present in your soil and root growth preparations will only improve the health and growth of your tree if the fungi are absent.

SALT DAMAGE can occur with the overuse of inorganic fertilizers or when road salt runs off into tree root zones. You'll notice leaves of affected trees with dried brown margins. If your soil is well drained, you may be able to wash the salts out with large volumes of water, but direct the runoff away from other trees by regrading or with barriers.

ROOT COMPACTION removes the pore space that holds oxygen. If construction equipment will be operating in the area, always protect tree roots by placing a fence around the root zone.

CHANGING GRADE LEVELS can kill trees. Lowering the grade cuts off feeder roots, dries out others, and removes nutrient-rich topsoil. Raising the grade with a blanket of new soil, on the other hand, reduces the diffusion of oxygen into the root zone. And sensitive trees like white oak can be killed by a grade change of as little as 2 inches.

To protect the tree when the grade is raised, you must create a tree well at the drip line. This protects the tree roots. Bricks or masonry retain the filled soil, and the soil must be layered with fabric and coarse gravel to allow for drainage. Also, you need to incorporate some form of pipe (usually PVC pipe) to allow for drainage and soil aeration within the well.

If the grade is lowered, the opposite is done; a wall is built around the tree, retaining the soil, and the same consideration for drainage must be allowed, again usually with a system of pipes.

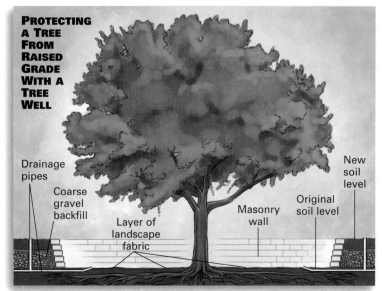

PROTECTING A TREE FROM RAISED GRADE WITH A TREE WELL

Drainage pipes — Coarse gravel backfill — Layer of landscape fabric — Masonry wall — Original soil level — New soil level

When raising the level of the soil around an established tree, it is essential to protect the root zone with a tree well at the drip line.

TREATING TRUNK WOUNDS

Injuries can occur to tree trunks even with the best precautions. Trunks can be damaged by machinery, by gnawers (mice, rabbits, and deer), by storms, and by children.

Prompt action is the key in treating trunk wounds. Cut away only the dead and injured bark; do not cut into healthy tissue. Spray with clean water. Apply moist sphagnum moss over the area and place a strip of white plastic to shade the wood. Remove it in two to three weeks. Do not apply wound dressings; they have only limited value.

TREE PROFESSIONALS

A good arborist offers a wide range of services—up-to-date pest and disease-control information, pruning advice, and tips for bracing and fertilizing. Remember the value of your established trees and choose a reputable, competent arborist. Referrals from friends and local nurseries are good indicators of quality. Be sure the arborist is adequately insured and get a written diagnosis, details of work to be performed, and a total cost estimate. When possible, choose a company certified by the International Society of Arboriculture (ISA). A list is available from the International Society of Arboriculture, Box 3129, Champaign, IL 61826.

TREE
SELECTION AND
GROWING GUIDE

Brilliant fall foliage and attractive winter bark are only two of the many reasons to select a tree. Shown above: Japanese maple (Acer japonicum 'Atropurpureum') and paper birch (Betula papyrifera).

Following are about 150 of the best and hardiest trees that grow well in the U.S. When reviewing the selections, choose the best tree for your specific conditions. A popular phrase which describes this process is "right plant, right place." A tree located improperly in the landscape will not be attractive and healthy—it will struggle and suffer.

Begin by creating a list of the features that you desire in the landscape (fall color, shade for the patio, screening, for example). Next, compare these characteristics with the features listed for each selection. As you consider each tree, many will be eliminated quickly, based on your criteria.

The short list of possibilities that you create for each location can be further refined by considering hardiness zone, growth rate, mature size, and landscape uses. The remaining sections will provide additional information to finalize your choice.

Also, look around your region. If you see an attractive tree that you'd like in your yard, find out what it is. Visit botanical gardens, arboretums, and garden centers.

If you've made your final choice, actively seek out examples of the tree in your region. If you can't find any, it could mean that you've stumbled on an underused tree for your region, but it might also mean that you've chosen a tree that doesn't work well there.

Finally, don't limit your options when choosing trees. If you have two or more possibilities, you can find bargains or switch to a second choice if the nursery is out of stock.

In this guide, we're going to give you the information that you need to make the best decision for your conditions. First, we give you the scientific and common name. This is important; different trees sometime share the same common name, and sometimes a tree has a number of common names. But if you know the scientific name, which is unique, you can make sure you're getting the right tree.

Just beneath the scientific name and common name, you'll see a silhouette of the shape of the tree, with its size at 20 years. Beside this, we've bulleted the most important facts about the tree, for easy browsing at a glance. We've also included here the hardiness of the tree and the growth rate.

In the main text, we tell you where the tree is from, its eventual size, and then recommend design uses and siting considerations. If a tree has piqued your interest, this information will help you narrow down your choices.

Finally, we will let you know of related species and cultivars, as well as the pros and cons of each. And because many trees are extensively hybridized, this will extend your range of choices even more.

Don't forget the growing information as you move through this guide. For years to come, we hope these specific suggestions will help you not only to pick your best trees but will also help you to make them healthy and long lived.

ABIES CONCOLOR

AY-bees CON-kah-lar

White fir

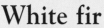

- Graceful, silver-blue, evergreen needles
- Pyramidal growth habit
- Dense, medium-textured foliage
- Growth rate: slow to medium, 6 to 9 inches per year
- Zones 4 to 8

Few trees exhibit the style, grace, and striking foliage of the white fir. Native to the western mountain states, it also grows well in the Midwest and East. It can grow up to 100 feet tall with age.

USES: Use it as a screening plant, as the tallest step in a layered design, or in groups. Its foliage color and texture create a nice contrast with the greens of deciduous trees and shrubs.

SITING AND CARE: Plant in full sun on well-drained or sloping terrain; does not tolerate wet soils. At the south edge of its range, keep the soil evenly moist. Inspect periodically for spider mites. Prune only diseased or broken branches.

RECOMMENDED VARIETIES:
'Candicans' is a narrow upright tree with large bright silver-blue needles. 'Compacta' is a dwarf tree with bright blue needles.

RELATED SPECIES:
Abies balsamea (balsam fir, zones 3 to 6). Native to Canada and the Great Lakes states, balsam fir is a valuable specimen tree, dark green with a silver overtone. Its narrow, upright form offers a strong vertical element and is ideal as a living Christmas tree (although it does not hold its needles as long as other firs). Balsam fir is adapted to cold climates, tolerates light shade, and prefers well-drained, moist, acidic soils. It is susceptible to several pests including canker diseases, spruce budworm, and spruce wooly aphid.
A. lasiocarpa (Rocky Mountain fir, zones 3 to 7). Native from Alaska to New Mexico. The variety *arizonica* is slow growing, with silvery blue-green foliage. The selection 'Compacta' is dwarf, making a striking specimen in the Midwest and East, but the northern species type does not do as well in the East.
A. nordmanniana (Nordmann fir, zones 5 to 8). Native to Asia Minor and the Mediterranean region, this fir is handsome and stately, with shiny, dark green needles with

silvery undersides. Useful as a screen or windbreak, it is relatively heat tolerant.
Abies procera (noble fir, zones 5 to 6). Native to the Pacific Northwest, its pyramidal shape and narrow form produce a striking accent in the landscape. Noble fir grows best in cool, moist areas, in well-drained soil, and it grows at a slow to medium rate. Its growth rate is a bit slower outside its native area. 'Glauca' has interesting, light blue foliage with a silvery cast.

White fir (A. concolor)

Blue noble fir (A. procera 'Glauca')

Nordmann fir (A. nordmanniana)

Noble fir (A. procera)

The firs offer a wide range of climatic tolerance, shapes, and sizes to the landscape. Many are available in silvery forms, their stiff, blue-green needles good for a contrast in the garden. Also, because their upright, pyramidal form is attractive in itself, they make good specimens as well.

ACER GINNALA

AY-sir ginn-ALL-uh

Amur maple

10'
8'

- Brilliant red fall color
- Bright red summer samaras (fruit)
- Graceful small habit
- Growth rate: medium, 10 to 12 inches per year
- Zones 3 to 8

Amur maple is ideal for small spaces, such as patios and front entrances.

A sturdy tree for the small front yard, Amur maple is native to China and Japan. It will eventually grow to 20 feet tall and wide.
USES: Ideal for patio gardens, courtyards, and containers, Amur maple adds texture and year-round interest to any small landscape.
SITING AND CARE: Tolerant of dry and alkaline soils. Allow clump to grow naturally, removing only aberrant growth.
RECOMMENDED VARIETIES: 'Flame' grows as a dense small tree or large shrub and has red fruits and red fall color.

Summer effect of Amur maple

ACER GRISEUM

AY-sir GRIH-zee-um

Paperbark maple

10'
5'

- Reddish brown, naturally peeling bark
- Spectacular red fall color, especially in the East
- Growth rate: slow, 4 to 6 inches per year
- Rounded, open habit
- Zones 5 to 7

The richly colored peeling bark of paperbark maple is especially showy in winter.

A good-looking specimen tree, its slow growth, rounded shape, and moderate size make it ideal for small landscapes. Native to western and central China. Will reach 20 to 30 feet tall and wide.
USES: A fine front-yard tree for the residential landscape, paperbark maple offers year-round interest—dark green leaves turning an impressive red (in most areas) in the fall, and a most distinctive, cinnamon-brown, curling, exfoliating bark. It has enough impact to be used in island plantings or as a centerpiece surrounded by large shrubs.
SITING AND CARE: Grows best in full sun but tolerates light shade. Mulch under tree to help reduce grass competition.
RELATED SPECIES: The closely related threeflower maple, *A. triflorum*, also has interesting curling bark, but less spectacular than *A. griseum*. It is somewhat faster growing and gaining in popularity in zones 5 to 7.

Fast-growing box elder is valuable as a temporary tree to fill space. Inset: 'Flamingo'

ACER NEGUNDO

AY-sir neh-GUN-do

Box elder

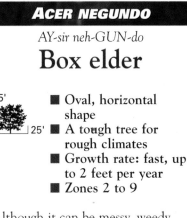
25'
25'

- Oval, horizontal shape
- A tough tree for rough climates
- Growth rate: fast, up to 2 feet per year
- Zones 2 to 9

Although it can be messy, weedy, and short-lived, boxelder thrives in the Canadian plains, the Dakotas, western Nebraska, and eastern Colorado, where other choices can be limited. And it is a fast grower as well. Native to Canada and the eastern United States. It can reach 65 feet tall.
USES: Useful as a temporary tree until more slow-growing trees are established. It is also a good choice for a windbreak in cold climates.
SITING AND CARE: Adaptable to light or medium shade; often found near creek banks. Boxelder requires no special care, and will grow in most sites.
RECOMMENDED VARIETIES AND RELATED SPECIES: 'Flamingo' has showy, variegated pink and green leaves with white borders. 'Variegatum' has variegated green-and-white leaves.

ACER PALMATUM

AY-sir pall-MAY-tum

Japanese maple

- Blazing fall foliage
- Elegant, sculptural, spreading form
- Medium-fine texture
- Growth rate: slow, averaging 4 to 6 inches per year
- Zones 5 to 8, depending on cultivar

While a must for the Japanese-style garden, this gorgeous tree adds appeal to any landscape. Native to Japan, China, and Korea. Can grow to 25 feet tall and as wide with age.
USES: Japanese maple offers striking color, form, and texture, and is ideal as an accent or in groupings and shrub borders.
SITING AND CARE: Grows best in morning sun, filtered shade in the afternoon, and cool, moist, mulched soil. Prune only to retain natural shape.

RECOMMENDED VARIETIES AND RELATED SPECIES:

Cultivars are numerous. 'Atropurpureum' and 'Bloodgood' have deep reddish purple leaves, red flowers, and fruit. 'Sango Kaku' has coral-colored stems and yellow leaves in fall. The dissectum types (laceleaf Japanese maples), have many threadlike leaves.

Japanese maple is available as many cultivars. Shown here is the popular 'Atropurpureum' in fall color.

Laceleaf Japanese maple

'Sangu-kaku' has bright coral bark.

'Bloodgood' has dark red leaves

Japanese maple in summer

ACER PLATANOIDES

AY-sir plat-uh-NOY-deez

Norway maple

- Large, thick leaves cast dense shade
- Yellow fall color
- Attractive ridged bark
- Growth rate: medium, 10 to 15 inches per year
- Zones 3 to 7

This maple offers deep green foliage and is native to Europe, from Norway to Switzerland. Can grow to 40 feet tall and 65 feet wide.
USES: Produces a beautiful upright oval shape and dense shade. Good street tree.
SITING AND CARE: Spreads out to 30 feet or more, so give it plenty of room. Protect the bark from sunscald, and prune only to retain its natural shape.
RECOMMENDED VARIETIES:
'Emerald Queen' has upright branches, dark green leaves, and an oval to round growth habit.

'Cleveland' has deep green leaves in summer, yellow in fall, and an upright oval habit. 'Deborah' has brilliant red emerging foliage. 'Summershade' is a rapid grower with an upright habit. 'Crimson King' and 'Royal Red' have very dark red foliage all summer. 'Crimson Sentry' is similar to 'Crimson King' but much narrower. 'Deborah' and 'Fairview' have dark red foliage in early summer, fading to green by fall. 'Drummondii' has white-margined leaves.

'Schwedleri' (above) is a very dark-leaved cultivar. Norway maple (right) has yellow fall color and a tall, oval structure.

Attractive as a young tree, red maple will grow quite large.

ACER RUBRUM

AY-sir ROO-brum

Red maple

- Outstanding red color in fall
- Upright, rounded growth habit
- Growth rate: medium to fast, 12 to 15 inches per year
- Zones 3 to 9

A good shade tree with excellent fall color, red maple is native to the east coast, from the Deep South north to New England. Grows to 50 feet tall and 40 feet wide.

USES: Red maple is a fine shade tree. Locate it near the southwest corner of a home for shade or in the back for framing views from indoors. **SITING AND CARE:** Plant in sun in rich, well-drained soil. Prune only to retain its natural shape. **RECOMMENDED VARIETIES AND RELATED SPECIES:** Acer × freemanii, freeman maple, a hybrid of silver and red maples, grows faster than red maple, slower than silver maple, with gray bark and red fall color. 'Jeffersred' (Autumn Blaze®) has a broad oval crown and orange-red fall color. 'Indian Summer' has an oval to rounded crown with red fall color; it is a vigorous grower, but not heat resistant.

A fast-growing tree, silver maple's weak wood and extensive roots can sometimes be troublesome.

ACER SACCHARINUM

AY-sir sack-uh-RYE-num

Silver maple

- Good for rapid effect
- Beware of greedy surface roots and weak wood
- Prolific seed producer
- Growth rate: fast, 12 to 20 inches per year
- Zones 3 to 9

A tree for wide open spaces, such as parks and acreages. Native to the eastern half of the U.S. Grows to 100 feet tall and 70 feet wide.

USES: Silver maple offers fast growth and shade for home lawn landscapes. It is best used in open areas, but not close to power lines, drainage or septic lines, and sidewalks. **SITING AND CARE:** Grows best in cool, moist, well-drained soils but will tolerate a wide variety of soil conditions. **RECOMMENDED VARIETIES:** 'Silver Queen' has an upright oval form and bears few fruit. 'Blair' grows with stronger branch angles than the species type. 'Skinneri' (Skinner's Cutleaf) has deeply cut leaves and a stronger framework than most silver maples.

ACER SACCHARUM

AY-sir sah-KAIR-um

✳Sugar maple

Well known for its flaming fall color, sugar maple has an attractive upright shape as well.

- Brilliant yellow, orange, or red fall color
- Superb shade tree
- Upright to oval growth habit
- Growth rate: medium, 10 to 15 inches per year
- Zones 4 to 7

A stately, elegant tree for shade or a tire swing, sugar maple is native from eastern Canada to the Great Lakes and south to Georgia. Grows 80 feet tall and 60 feet wide. **USES:** Its beautiful fall color and great shade make it an outstanding choice for large backyards and for open areas.

SITING AND CARE: Not tolerant of compacted soils or of small or restricted root zones. Mulch regularly to help keep the roots cool and moist during the period of establishment. **RECOMMENDED VARIETIES:** 'Green Mountain' has thick, deep green foliage with good scorch resistance. 'Bonfire' is a vigorous grower with an oval habit. 'Green Column' has an upright, columnar shape and yellow-orange leaves in the fall. 'Legacy' is drought resistant and has thick, heavy leaves. 'Flax Mill Majesty' is fast growing and broadly oval, a well-shaped tree even when young, with red-orange autumn foliage.

AESCULUS X CARNEA

ESS-kuh-luss car-NEE-uh

Red horsechestnut

20'
15'

- Bright red flowers in early summer
- Stately, rounded growth habit
- Deep green foliage
- Growth rate: medium, 10 to 12 inches per year
- Zones 4 to 8

This is a hybrid between *Aesculus hippocastanum* and the red buckeye

(*A. pavia*), a small tree from the south-central United States. Grows to 40 feet tall and 30 feet wide.
USES: Good for large yards, red horsechestnut is an excellent accent in open areas. Its deep green foliage contrasts nicely with lighter shrubs and dwarf evergreens.
SITING AND CARE: Grows best in deep, rich, moist soils.
RECOMMENDED VARIETIES AND RELATED SPECIES: 'Briotii' has 10-inch red flowers and dark green leaves; tolerates urban conditions fairly well. This is the most widely available cultivar of red horsechestnut. *A. pavia* (red buckeye) grows to only 20 to 25 feet tall, with impressive, deep red,

tubular flowers in early summer. Hardy in zones 5 to 9.

Though it starts out with a pyramidal structure, red horsechestnut eventually grows into a rounded shape.

AESCULUS GLABRA

ESS-kuh-luss GLAY-bra

Ohio buckeye

20'
15'

- Large, spreading growth habit
- Fragrant yellowish-white flowers in early summer
- Growth rate: medium, 10 to 12 inches per year
- Zones 3 to 7

Its 2-inch beige, warty fruit adds color, texture, and interest. Native to the Ohio River Valley. It can reach 40 feet tall by 30 feet wide.

USES: This buckeye offers nice rounded growth habit and shade but is not a tree for limited spaces. Give it a large open area for proper root development.
SITING AND CARE: Does not tolerate extreme drought. Keep roots cool and moist with mulch. Inspect for spider mites and leaf scorch in dry sites.
RELATED SPECIES: *A. flava* (yellow or sweet buckeye) is a larger version of *A. glabra*, about the same size as *A. hippocastanum*. It is used mostly in its native range, from the Central Plains to Georgia, where it makes a fine large shade tree more troublefree than *A. hippocastanum*.

The bright green leaves of this Ohio buckeye are a good sign that the tree is healthy in its site.

AESCULUS HIPPOCASTANUM

ESS-kuh-luss hih-poh-CASS-tuh-num

Common horsechestnut

20'
15'

- Pyramidal, rounded growth habit and great size at maturity
- Leaves compound and 5 to 9 inches long
- Growth rate: medium, 7 to 10 inches per year
- Zone 3 to 7

This large tree has large leaves and

white flowers in early summer, and is native to the mountains of Greece and Albania. Grows 55 to 70 feet tall, with a similar spread.
USES: Common horsechestnut is a good tree for large areas and adds color, texture, and interest to acreages, estates, and larger backyards. It is not for the small residential landscape.
SITING AND CARE: Locate it in full sun or light shade. Avoid dry conditions. Horsechestnut is often badly disfigured by a leaf-blotch disease in addition to leaf scorch from drought.
RECOMMENDED VARIETIES: 'Baumannii' has long lasting, showy flowers but does not bear fruit.

An impressive tree when in flower, common horsechestnut needs some room to grow and spread.

ALBIZIA JULIBRISSIN

awl-BIH-zee-uh ju-lih-BRISS-in

Silk tree or Mimosa

Mimosa's problems are often forgiven because of its feathery foliage and distinctive flowers.

12' — 15'

- Pink, brush-like flowers in summer
- Wide-spreading, umbrellalike canopy
- Ferny, fine-textured foliage lends tropical effect
- Growth rate: medium to fast, 8 to 12 inches per year
- Zones 6 to 9

With exotic flowers and ferny foliage, mimosa offers a distinct tropical feel. Native to Asia, from Iran to China. Reaches 25 to 40 feet tall and wider than it is tall.

USES: In mass plantings or on hillsides away from residential settings, its fast growth produces a rapid tropical effect. However, its susceptibility to vascular wilt disease limits its usefulness.

SITING AND CARE: Allow it to grow naturally in a multitrunked form. When disease or occasional winterkill limits growth, prune severely to produce regrowth. Will usually come back after winterkill. Because flowers drop and limbs often break, keep it away from sidewalks or patios, where it might cause a serious litter problem. It can also seed aggressively.

RECOMMENDED VARIETIES: 'Charlotte' and 'Tryon' are wilt-resistant, but seldom available in the landscape industry.

ALNUS GLUTINOSA

AWL-nuss gloo-tih-NOH-suh

European black alder

If your yard or planting area is too wet for most trees, common alder will probably be right at home.

30' — 15'

- Tolerant of wet soils
- Upright to slightly pyramidal habit
- Dark green glossy leaves in summer
- Growth rate: fast when young, slows to a moderate 12 to 15 inches per year
- Zones 4 to 8

Alder is an ideal medium to large tree for low wet spots in the landscape (where most other trees fail), and is native to most areas of Europe. Reaches 40 to 60 feet tall and 20 to 40 feet wide.

USES: A good choice for landscapes with streams, alder can also be grown as an understory tree. It is frequently found naturalized along waterways and does quite well in residential lawns if properly sited. It is considered one of the best trees for a wet site.

SITING AND CARE: Avoid planting near sidewalks and sewer lines. Very tolerant: grow in full sun to full shade. Mildew and leaf rust can be problems in rainy seasons.

RECOMMENDED VARIETIES: 'Aurea' has golden yellow leaves. 'Imperialis' has deeply cut lobes on light green leaves; 'Pyramidalis' displays a pyramidal to upright form. Cultivars can be hard to find; usually sold only as the species.

AMELANCHIER X GRANDIFLORA

ah-mih-LAN-kee-er grand-i-FLOR-uh

Apple serviceberry

Like redbud, apple serviceberry is a tough, small native tree that signals spring with flowers before its leaves.

20' — 20'

- White flowers emerge in spring before leaves
- Red to purple fruit, attractive to birds
- Elegant small tree or large shrub
- Growth rate: medium, 10 to 15 inches per year
- Zones 3 to 8

Growing well in most of the East or Midwest, serviceberry is a versatile tree for the landscape and is loved by birds and humans. Grows to 35 feet tall and 30 feet wide.

USES: Incorporate serviceberry into front-yard landscape beds or islands, courtyards, and patios or in windbreaks for wildlife habitat. Its flowers, fruit, and silvery gray bark contrast well with nearby perennials and ground covers.

SITING AND CARE: Prefers well-drained, moist soils.

RECOMMENDED VARIETIES AND RELATED SPECIES: 'Autumn Brilliance' has orange to red fall leaf color and abundant fruit. Has many other excellent cultivars. *Amelanchier arborea* (downy serviceberry) is a single or multistemmed tree to 60 feet high with a rounded crown. *Amelanchier laevis* (Allegheny serviceberry) is a large shrub with bronze emerging foliage; its fruit is sweet, deep purple, and favored by birds.

ASIMINA TRILOBA

ay-SIM-ih-nuh trye-LOH-buh

Pawpaw

15'
8'

- Large, tropical-looking leaves
- Small multitrunked tree or large shrub
- Produces delicious fruit with the flavor of banana custard
- Tolerant of shade
- Growth rate: medium, 8 to 12 inches per year
- Good yellow fall foliage
- Zones 5 to 8

Pawpaw is loved by humans and wildlife alike. It is native to the East, from New York to Florida, but will grow west to Missouri. Older trees can reach 30 feet tall and 20 feet wide.

USES: Allow it to grow in masses for wildlife and conservation value and to promote diversity in the landscape. This tree favors moist woodland sites but is also adaptable to semishade, woodland, or understory conditions.

SITING AND CARE: Locate it in loose, fertile, woodland soil and grow it without shaping to allow it to form large thickets, or prune it carefully to train it as a pyramidal tree with a single trunk.

An underappreciated native tree, pawpaw offers edible fruit, distinctive leaves, and fall color.

BETULA NIGRA

BET-yoo-luh NYE-gruh

River birch

30'
20'

- Peeling, cinnamon-brown bark
- Pyramidal to oval growth habit
- Growth rate: medium to fast, 15 to 20 inches per year
- Zones 4 to 9

A versatile, large tree, this birch fits in most landscapes. It is a Midwest native, growing from Minnesota and Kansas, east to New England. Grows to 50 to 70 feet tall.

USES: Its uses are multitudinous: as a shade tree, in large landscape beds, or massed alongside stream banks. Resistance to bronze birch borer is a real plus.

SITING AND CARE: Grows best in acid, moist soils and adapts to full sun or partial shade. Keep roots cool with a ground cover. Prune only low-hanging branches.

RECOMMENDED VARIETIES AND RELATED SPECIES: 'Cully' (Heritage®) bark ages pink and brown. *Betula lenta* (cherry birch, zones 4 to 7) is native to Appalachia. It has beautiful yellow fall foliage color and lustrous, reddish-brown bark similar to cherry.

River birch is a native of flood plains, and has beautiful peeling bark when young.

BETULA PENDULA

BET-yoo-luh PEN-dyoo-luh

European white birch

25'
12'

- Outstanding white bark, dashes of black
- Yellow fall foliage
- Upright pyramidal form
- Growth rate: medium to fast, 12 to 15 inches per year
- Zones 3 to 6

Superb for rapid-effect groves in cool-summer areas. Native to

Europe and northern Asia. Occasionally reaches 60 feet.

USES: Soften a corner of the yard, or use it as a screen or background. Bark color and branch texture make it an excellent medium-sized tree.

SITING AND CARE: Needs moist but well-drained soil. Grow ground cover to keep roots cool. Tolerates light shade. Drought and heat stress invite birch borer.

RECOMMENDED VARIETIES AND RELATED SPECIES: Cutleaved, columnar, and weeping cultivars are available. *Betula papyrifera* (Paper Birch), exhibits delightful stark white bark and its dark-green leaves turn yellow in the fall. Subject to heat stress and

borers in hot climates but slightly less than *B. pendula*. 'Whitespire,' (zones 4-5.) is resistant to borers, good for the Midwest.

When European white birch colors in the fall, it lights up the landscape all around it.

With the right climate and conditions, lemon bottlebrush will bloom year round.

CALLISTEMON CITRINUS

kal-ih-STEE-mon sih-TRY-nuss

Lemon bottlebrush

10'

10'

- Bright red bottlebrush flowers nearly all year in mild climates
- Upright in habit; rounded crown shape
- Stems and leaves produce citrus odor when bruised
- Growth rate: fast, 10 to 15 inches per year
- Zones 9 to 10

Tolerant of southern heat and drought, and a favorite in California. With age it reaches 20 to 25 feet high.

USES: Excellent as a specimen, hedge or screen. Makes an interesting espalier. In northern climates grow it in large containers and bring it indoors in winter.

SITING AND CARE: Best in moist, well-drained soils in full sun. Tolerant of many soil types and extreme temperatures.

RECOMMENDED VARIETIES AND RELATED SPECIES: 'Splendens' has glossy, bright-red flowers that are larger than those of the species. Other species of Callistemon are useful in California.

C. betulus 'Fastigiata' offers a tall, upright form for use either as a specimen or a screen (right).

CARPINUS BETULUS

car-PYE-nuss BET-yoo-luss

European hornbeam

15'

15'

- Regular, oval habit is good for formal effects
- Growth rate: slow to medium, 10 to 12 inches per year
- Zones 5 to 7

This medium-size tree does well in a wide range of conditions. Native to Europe and Asia Minor. Reaches 40 feet at maturity.

USES: European hornbeam is suitable in urban landscapes, for screens, for street plantings, and in residential lawns.

SITING AND CARE: Grows best in full sun but tolerates light shade.

RECOMMENDED VARIETIES AND RELATED SPECIES: 'Fastigiata' grows in an upright form, 35 to 45 feet tall. 'Globosa' is rounded with foliage masses. *Carpinus caroliniana* (American hornbeam; zones 3 to 9) is a small to medium upright tree, with dark green foliage that turns yellow to orange and scarlet in fall, and twisted, muscular trunks and branches effective in winter. Its size lends itself to smaller landscapes.

Besides offering edible nuts, pecan matures into a majestic tree.

CARYA ILLINOINENSIS

CARE-ee-uh ill-ih-noy-YEN-siss

Pecan

25'

20'

- Large, stately tree with a wide spreading habit
- Grown for edible nuts, or as a shade tree in parklike settings
- Growth rate: slow to moderate, usually 10 to 12 inches per year
- Zones 6 to 9

A famous tree, mainly because of its edible nuts, pecan nevertheless can be used in the landscape. Its open,

upright habit allows turf growth underneath the wide-spreading branches, but it drops much nut, leaf, and twig litter. Will grow to 100 feet tall and almost as wide.

USES: Pecan is a good tree for parks and large residential lots; not for smaller lots. Expect squirrels.

SITING AND CARE: Requires a large open space; can grow to 80 feet or more. Prune to maintain central leader. Insects and diseases are seldom serious problems except for inhibiting nut production.

CATALPA BIGNONIOIDES

kuh-TALL-puh big-noh-nee-OY-deez

Southern catalpa

15'
15'

- Large, fast-growing tree with bold texture
- White flowers cover the tree canopy in early summer
- Long, narrow seedpods are a litter problem
- Growth rate: fast, 12 to 15 inches per year
- Zones 5 to 9

Southern catalpa is a medium-sized tree often associated with old-fashioned landscapes. It is native to the south-central United States. With age, it can reach 40 feet tall and wide.

USES: Can be used for fast shade in open spaces. Not well suited to the front-yard residential landscape; best in background settings.

SITING AND CARE: This tough tree requires little care and adapts well to a wide range of sites.

RECOMMENDED VARIETIES AND RELATED SPECIES: 'Aurea' has rich, yellow leaves. 'Nana' has a dwarf, bushy form that is usually grafted on a standard rootstock. These can be hard to find. *C. speciosa* (Northern catalpa, zones 4 to 8) flowers two weeks earlier.

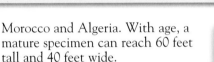

A fast-growing, tough shade tree, southern catalpa can surprise you with its showy, trumpet-shaped flowers.

CEDRUS LIBANI SSP. ATLANTICA

SEE-druss lih-BAH-nye

Atlas cedar

20'
10'

- Conical when young, large, flat-topped and picturesque with age
- Blue-green needles
- Growth rate: moderately slow, 10 to 12 inches a year, slowing with age
- Zones 6 to 9

Resistant to drought and requiring very little maintenance, Atlas cedar is native to the Atlas Mountains of Morocco and Algeria. With age, a mature specimen can reach 60 feet tall and 40 feet wide.

USES: Place this specimen tree in the landscape where it can shine, with complementary-colored shrubs planted nearby, keeping in mind the ultimate size of the tree.

SITING AND CARE: Prefers full sun but can grow in partial shade.

RECOMMENDED VARIETIES AND RELATED SPECIES: 'Glauca' has bright blue needles, similar to clones of Colorado blue spruce. This is the cultivar usually seen in landscapes. *C. libani* (Cedar of Lebanon) is also a fine accent tree. Hardiest cultivars are useful in warmer areas of zone 5.

A majestic specimen tree, the bluish foliage of Atlas cedar blends well with many garden colors.

CELTIS OCCIDENTALIS

SELL-tiss ock-sih-den-TAL-iss

Common hackberry

25'
20'

- Rough, tough tree for difficult places
- Upright, round shape
- Branches tend to droop with an arching habit
- Growth rate: medium to fast, 12 to 15 inches per year
- Zones 4 to 8

Although it is a bit coarse and rough looking, hackberry will grow in dry and windy sites in the plains and prairie states, and is a substitute for American elm in those areas. Grows to 80 to 100 feet in a good site with fertile soil.

USES: Makes a good shade or street tree in residential settings, if not sited too close to the house.

SITING AND CARE: Grows in moderately wet or dry soils and requires very little care. Hackberry nipplegall is a harmless insect that inhabits the leaves.

RECOMMENDED VARIETIES: 'Prairie Pride' has leathery foliage and is upright and fast growing.

Often considered a "rough" tree, common hackberry nevertheless possesses a rugged charm.

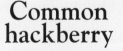

Katsura tree's foliage emerges purplish, matures to bluish green, and often colors brightly in the fall.

CERCIDIPHYLLUM JAPONICUM

sir-sih-dih-FYE-lum juh-PAW-nih-kum

Katsura tree

20'

12'

- Graceful spreading growth habit; single or multiple trunks
- Emerging reddish foliage changes to soft blue-green
- Some trees develop pinkish to red autumn foliage
- Growth rate: medium, 12 to 14 inches per year
- Zones 5 to 8

A tree with many fine attributes if properly sited, this tree has interesting, heart-shaped leaves and a moderate growth rate. A graceful and stately tree, katsura tree is native to Japan and China. Grows to 60 feet tall and sometimes wider.

USES: This is a medium to large tree, full and dense even when young, and a good choice for creating dappled shade.

SITING AND CARE: Best in full sun to part shade and moist, well-drained soil. Provide additional moisture during periods of drought.

RECOMMENDED VARIETIES: 'Pendula' is a cultivar with a weeping form whose height can vary from 20 to 50 feet.

Eastern redbud is beloved for its cheerful purple-pink flowers in spring and attractive, open form.

CERCIS CANADENSIS

SIR-siss can-uh-DEN-siss

Eastern redbud

12'

12'

- Pink-purple flowers open in spring before the heart-shaped leaves emerge
- Zigzag branch pattern in winter
- Growth rate: medium, 6 to 10 inches per year
- Zones 3 to 9

This is a versatile small tree that provides interest throughout most of the year. It is native to the eastern

and central United States. It can grow 25 to 35 feet tall and wide.

USES: This is an excellent front-yard tree to accent shrub borders, soften harsh corners, or to use as an understory tree near larger, established shade trees.

SITING AND CARE: Tolerates shade, but best with some sun. Protect trunk and bark from damage, which can lead to cankers.

RECOMMENDED VARIETIES: 'Forest Pansy' is a purple-leaved type that needs shade in warmer climates. 'Alba' and 'Royal White' have white flowers. 'Flame' has semi-double purple-pink flowers. 'Pinkbud' and 'Wither's Pink Charm' have clear pink flowers.

Lawson false cypress offers many cultivars, some of which have golden foliage, like 'Golden Dwarf' here.

CHAMAECYPARIS LAWSONIANA

kam-uh-SIP-uh-ris law-so-nee-AY-nuh

Lawson false cypress

15'

5'

- Pyramidal shape, graceful appearance
- Evergreen screen
- Growth rate: slow, 6 to 10 inches a year
- Zones 6 to 8

An outstanding tree in the Pacific Northwest. Native to southern Oregon and northern California. Matures to 50 feet tall.

USES: Excellent as a specimen or for screening with lacy foliage and fibrous, red-brown bark.

SITING AND CARE: Best in well-drained, moist soils with wind protection, in light shade or in sun.

RECOMMENDED VARIETIES: Cultivars are numerous. 'Allumii' has blue-green foliage, and grows more rapidly than the species. 'Ellwoodii', a dwarf plant, grows slowly to 8 feet. 'Garden King' is columnar, 40 to 50 feet tall, with pendulous branch tips and golden foliage that turns bronze in winter. 'Oregon Blue' has blue foliage and grows to 50 feet tall. 'Silver Queen' is conical, to 30 feet tall, with variegated foliage.

CHIONANTHUS VIRGINICUS

kee-oh-NAN-thuss ver-JIN-uh-kuss

White fringe tree

10'

10'

- Clouds of fragrant, white, threadlike flowers in late spring
- Large, multistemmed shrub or small tree
- Light green foliage
- Growth rate: slow, 6 to 10 inches per year
- Zones 5 to 9

An excellent plant for use near buildings and in masses, white fringe tree is native to the Southeast. It reaches 20 to 30 feet tall and as wide or wider. Female plants bear blue-black fruit in late summer and fall. Foliage turns clear yellow in autumn in some years.

USES: Great for a patio garden, courtyard, the shrub border, and in a variety of locations in the landscape. The flowers can be quite attractive and refreshing to the passerby. Tolerant of many urban and street conditions.

SITING AND CARE: Plant in full sun. Grows well in moist, well-drained soils. Prune only to control aberrant growth.

RECOMMENDED VARIETIES: *C. retusus*, oriental fringetree, is larger and less hardy; zones 6 to 9.

White fringe tree flowers offer fragrance as well as beauty.

CINNAMOMUM CAMPHORA

sih-nah-MOH-mum KAM-foh-rah

Camphor tree

12'

8'

- Rounded growth habit and clean, fissured bark
- Bronze-red spring foliage turns shiny yellow-green in winter
- Growth rate: slow, 6 to 8 inches per year
- Zone 9 to 10

This attractive, evergreen shade tree grows to 50 feet tall and wide. With its handsome, changing foliage and pleasing, rounded shape, it has something to offer in all seasons. It is native to Japan and China.

USES: Camphor tree is a good street tree if given enough room, and it provides shade in all seasons. Its evergreen foliage is an effective background and contrasts well with lighter-colored plants, but the dense shade and surface-rooting tendency of this tree limit planting other specimens in close proximity; also, because of the rooting problem, avoid planting near sidewalks.

SITING AND CARE: Locate in full sun, allowing room on all sides. Mulch under drip line to limit evaporation and to keep area attractive. Not bothered by pests.

Camphor tree's neat habit and attractive bark give it a quiet appeal in the landscape.

CLADRASTIS LUTEA

kluh-DRASS-tiss LOO-tee-uh

Yellowwood

15'

15'

- Showy, white, heavily fragrant flowers borne in hanging chains in late spring
- Zigzag branching pattern evident in winter, accompanied by seedpods
- Lovely smooth bark
- Growth rate: slow to medium, 10 to 12 inches per year
- Zones 5 to 8

Yellowwood is a refined medium-size tree for restricted spaces. It is native to streamsides and river banks of the southeastern U.S. Clear yellow autumn foliage. Grows 30 to 35 feet tall and 20 to 25 feet wide.

USES: This is a nice tree for the rear corner of the residential backyard landscape bed. Use it as a shade tree on smaller properties and place it in larger areas alongside small trees or larger shrubs such as arrowwood or blackhaw viburnum.

SITING AND CARE: Best in sun to part shade and moist, well-drained soil. Prune in summer to avoid excessive sap bleeding. Pruning is usually only necessary to prevent poor or weak branch angles.

Strong muscular trunks are just part of the reason yellowwood is a beautiful year-round tree.

CORNUS FLORIDA

KORE-nuss FLO-rih-duh

Flowering dogwood

Normally white in bloom, flowering dogwood has several pink forms. Shown at top is C. florida 'Rubra'.

- Showy flower bracts emerge before the leaves in late spring
- Graceful horizontal branching, good fall color, and red fruit
- Growth rate: slow to medium, 10 to 12 inches per year, slower with age
- Zones 6 to 9 (zone 5, if northern seed sources are used)

Native to the eastern United States. Reaches 20 to 30 feet tall. It is most useful within its native range.

USES: Particularly effective in masses and in partial shade as an understory tree. Excellent for all-season appeal: summer foliage, spring flowers, fall color and fruit, and winter bark and branches.

SITING AND CARE: Keep roots cool to avoid leaf and trunk scorch. Use an acidifying fertilizer if in a higher pH area. Anthracnose disease is devastating. Lawn mower damage to trunks provides almost certain entry for this disease.

RECOMMENDED VARIETIES:
'Barton White', 'Cherokee Princess', 'Cloud 9', and 'Fragrant Cloud' are good selections for form and early white flowers. 'Barton White' is reputed to be resistant to anthracnose disease. 'Cherokee Chief' and 'Rubra' are pink-flowering forms, 'Welch's Junior Miss' has bicolored pink and white flowering bracts, and is one of the few cultivars that perform well on the Gulf Coast (zone 9). There are also selections with pink-, white-, or yellow-variegated leaves.

'Gold Nugget' (left), flowering dogwood fruits (above right), and 'Welchii' (near right)

CORNUS KOUSA

KORE-nuss KOO-suh

Kousa dogwood

'Chanticleer' (top), fall foliage of 'Lustgarten Weeping' (above), and pink flowers of 'Satomi' (lower left)

- White-bracted flowers bloom 2 to 3 weeks later than *Cornus florida*
- Open, horizontal-branching habit
- Beautiful flaking bark, red fleshy fruits, outstanding fall foliage color
- Resistant to pests that trouble C. *florida*
- Growth rate: slow when young, 8 to 10 inches per year
- Zones 5 to 8

A tree with tremendous impact and appeal in all seasons. Native to Japan and Korea. Grows to 20 feet.

USES: A natural for courtyards or for softening harsh corners of buildings. Grows robustly without impeding surrounding plants.

SITING AND CARE: Best in well-drained soils. Can grow in full sun but does better in partial shade, growing into its natural, open shape. Thrives with some protection from sun and wind.

RECOMMENDED VARIETIES AND RELATED SPECIES:
'Chanticleer' has white flowers and strongly horizontal branching. 'Lustgarten Weeping' has a graceful weeping form. C. × *rutgersensis* represents hybrids between C. *florida* and C. *kousa*, developed at Rutgers University. Faster growing than C. *kousa*, the cultivars in this group are known to be resistant to anthracnose and dogwood borer; they are safe alternatives to C. *florida* in zones 6 to 8, and perhaps other zones as well. Their flowering season is about midway between C. *florida* and C. *kousa*. 'Rutban' (Aurora®), 'Rutcan', 'Rutdan' (Galaxy®), (Constellation®), and 'Rutlan' (Ruth Ellen®) are white-bracted clones in the C. × *rutgersensis* group; 'Rutgan' (Stellar Pink®) is a clone with pink bracts.

CRATAEGUS CRUS-GALLI

kruh-TEE-guss krooz-GALL-eye

Cockspur hawthorn

12'
12'

- White flowers in early spring
- Shiny dark leaves turn orange in fall
- Loads of bright red fruit fall into winter
- Small tree; graceful broad shape
- Growth rate: medium, 6 to 10 inches per year
- Zones 3 to 7

A versatile small tree with relatively few serious problems, its native range is from eastern Canada to Kansas and the Carolinas. Reaches 30 feet tall and wide.

USES: It can be trained into a tall hedge but is best as a single specimen in borders and at corners of buildings. Provides excellent definition and height in the shrub border. Tolerates urban conditions. Its ornamental fruit remains effective in late summer and fall and into winter.

SITING AND CARE: Full sun but can tolerate light shade. Leaf miner and aphids are minor pests. Fruit may be disfigured by cedar-apple rust if eastern red cedar (*Juniperus virginiana*) trees are nearby.

RECOMMENDED VARIETIES: 'Inermis' is thornless (important for homeowners with small children).

Cockspur hawthorn greets spring with a profusion of small white flowers.

The bright fruits offer a well-needed spot of color from late summer into winter.

CRATAEGUS PHAENOPYRUM

kruh-TEE-guss feh-NAW-puh-rum

Washington hawthorn

15'
10'

- Abundant white flowers in late spring and early summer, large clusters of scarlet fruit, good fall foliage
- Tough constitution
- Good for border and screens; formidable thorns
- Small with elegant, spreading habit
- Growth rate: medium; 10 to 12 inches per year
- Zones 3 to 8

Native from Virginia to Alabama and Missouri, this is one of the best hawthorns for fall fruiting and color—a hardy, versatile small tree for almost any landscape. Will grow to about 20 feet tall.

USES: Use as a single specimen, background for hedges, or in shrub borders. Parents of small children should be aware of the thorns.

SITING AND CARE: Locate in full sun or partial shade, accompanied by shrubs or other small trees. This species of hawthorn is very resistant to cedar-apple rust.

RECOMMENDED VARIETIES AND RELATED SPECIES: 'Vaughn', a hybrid between *C. crus-galli* and *C. phaenopyrum*, produces abundant fruit, which remain on the tree for much of the winter. It is broad and low (15 to 20 feet) and extremely thorny, which has limited its use. *C. × mordenensis* 'Toba' is a hybrid developed in the harsh climate of Manitoba, Canada. Its white flowers gradually turn rose, and produce few fruits. Almost thornless, 'Toba' is extremely cold hardy (zone 3) but is susceptible to cedar-apple rust. *Crataegus viridis* 'Winter King' is a broad vase-shaped tree, slightly larger than *C. phaenopyrum* (20 to 25 feet) and faster growing. Like other hawthorns, it is a tree for all seasons, with spring clusters of applelike flowers, followed by lustrous green leaves that change to purplish red in the fall, and distinctive silvery branches. It holds its fruit as long as *C. phaenopyrum*.

'Winter King' hawthorn (above) and Washington hawthorn (inset) both shine brightly in winter.

A strongly formal tree, Japanese cedar shows off well as a specimen in the landscape.

CRYPTOMERIA JAPONICA

krip-toh-MARE-ee-uh ja-PON-ih-kuh

Japanese cedar

15'

8'

- Formal, with textured evergreen foliage
- Upright, pyramidal growth habit
- Growth rate: medium to fast, 10 to 15 inches per year
- Zones 6 to 8

Japanese cedar is a good evergreen specimen tree for larger residential landscapes. Native to China and Japan. It eventually grows 50 to 60 feet tall.

USES: A good specimen tree for the corner of a large lot. Locate it in semiprotected sites, near other plant groupings.
SITING AND CARE: This tree does not tolerate drought well; water during drought.
RECOMMENDED VARIETIES: 'Yoshino' is relatively fast growing, and its bright green summer foliage bronzes slightly in winter. 'Lobbii' refers to a clone of mature form and foliage and probably differs little from the species type. There are also many dwarf, shrubby forms of this species from which to choose.

Leyland cypress readily lends itself to use as a specimen or as a sheared formal hedge.

CUPRESSOCYPARIS X LEYLANDII

koo-press-oh-SIP-uh-riss lay-LAWN-dee-eye

Leyland cypress

20'

5'

- Stately, graceful, horizontal branches; columnar form
- Dense evergreen
- Growth rate: fast, 1 to 3 feet per year
- Zones 7 to 10

This century-old hybrid between *Chamaecyparis nootkatensis* and *Cupressus macrocarpa* is vigorous in the extreme, screening quickly, then dominating landscapes until cut down. Reaches 70 feet tall.
USES: Useful as a specimen tree, for tall hedges, and for screening where there is ample space.
SITING AND CARE: Plant it in full sun. Tolerates many soil types and conditions. Protect the trunk from bruising to reduce the chances of canker disease.
RECOMMENDED VARIETIES: 'Naylor's Blue' is the bluest cultivar available and has a more open form. 'Castlewellan Gold' is slower growing, with yellow foliage, bronzing in winter. 'Leighton Green' is narrowly columnar, with bright green foliage.

CUPRESSUS SEMPERVIRENS

koo-PRESS-us sem-per-VYE-renz

Italian cypress

Because of its powerful verticality, only a few Italian cypress trees are needed to make a strong statement.

20'

4'

- Upright, very narrow, columnar form
- Dense, thick growth
- Growth rate: medium to fast, 1 to 2 feet per year
- Zones 7 to 9

A strong vertical line to balance horizontal architecture, and a must for formal gardens in mild climates. Native to southern Europe. Grows 30 to 40 feet tall and 3 to 6 feet wide.
USES: The ideal sentinel. A good screen if planted close together.
SITING AND CARE: Tolerates drought and a wide range of soils but is not tolerant of heavy, wet, or poorly drained soils.

RECOMMENDED VARIETIES AND RELATED SPECIES: 'Swane's Gold' is slow growing and columnar with golden green foliage. 'Glauca' has blue-green foliage. *Cupressus macrocarpa* (Monterey cypress) is a large tree that is upright when young, broad and spreading with age. Grows best on southern California's coast (to 40 feet). Humid areas in zones 7 to 9 are stressing and often result in disease. Most often used as a windbreak or clipped hedge. *Cupressus arizonica* (Arizona cypress) is a medium-size tree, 30 by 20 feet, with silvery blue evergreen foliage and reddish brown bark. Use as a windbreak or screen; best in the Southwest, zones 7 to 9.

DAVIDIA INVOLUCRATA

dah-VIH-dee-uh in-voh-LOO-cra-tuh

Dove tree

15'
10'

- Unusual flowers are effective in late spring
- Distinctly pyramidal
- Golfball-shaped fruit and orange-brown bark add winter interest
- Growth rate: slow to medium, 8 to 12 inches per year
- Zones 6 to 8

This unique, broadly pyramidal tree is native to the interior of China. It grows to 30 to 40 feet after about 50 years, and eventually taller.

USES: Best in medium- to large-sized lots as a handsome flowering specimen. While other flowering trees can look "busy" if planted nearby, dove tree is very effective with rhododendrons at its base.

SITING AND CARE: Adapted to full sun or partial shade. Grows well in a landscape bed with shrubs and perennials if mulched to keep the bed cool and moist. Prune as necessary to retain shape.

RECOMMENDED VARIETIES AND RELATED SPECIES: *D. vilmoriniana* has leaves that are more glaucous than the species and is slightly more cold hardy.

Renowned for its singular flowers, dove tree is considered one of the most spectacular flowering trees.

DIOSPYROS KAKI

dye-OSS-per-us KHA-kee

Japanese or Oriental persimmon

20'
12'

- Yellow to light-green spring leaves change to reddish orange in fall
- Edible fruit is showy on bare branches well into winter
- Growth rate: slow, 10 to 12 inches per year
- Zone 9

After changing color, the leaves drop a few weeks later, leaving the fruit clinging to the branches for long winter display. Native to China and Korea. Can reach 30 feet tall and wide.

USES: Use as a specimen or in a grove for multiseason effect.

SITING AND CARE: Best in full sun and well-drained soil. Needs periodic thinning in late winter for maximum fruit production. Keep roots evenly moist to avoid premature fruit drop.

RECOMMENDED VARIETIES: 'Chocolate' fruit is flecked brown, with very sweet flesh. 'Fuyu' has golden orange fruit with firm flesh and is very popular. 'Hachiya' has good ornamental qualities; it bears large fruit, and is sometimes seen in the produce section of markets.

As the golden fruits of Japanese persimmon 'Fuyu' ripen, the softly colored leaves change as well.

DIOSPYROS VIRGINIANA

dye-OSS-per-us ver-jih-nee-AY-nuh

Common persimmon

20'
12'

- Newly emerging bronze leaves turn lustrous dark green in summer
- Yellow to orange fruit ripens with the first hard frost, turning from sour to sweet
- Growth rate: slow, 10 to 12 inches per year
- Zones 5 to 9

One of the best fruit trees with ornamental qualities, this small tree (25 to 40 feet) is native to the eastern half of the U.S.

USES: Naturalize it in your home fruit garden as a border tree or one that separates the garden from the rest of the landscape. It is a great conversation piece. Don't plant it near paving or decks.

SITING AND CARE: Grows best in fertile soil, moist but well drained. Other than leaf spot, persimmon is relatively pest free.

RECOMMENDED VARIETIES: Good cultivars for habit and fruit are available from specialty growers.

The attractive furrowed bark of common persimmon extends its seasons of interest into winter.

ELAEAGNUS ANGUSTIFOLIA

ell-ee-AG-nuss an-gus-tih-FOH-lee-uh

Russian olive

Besides being a useful windbreak, Russian olive also offers a hard-to-find silvery gray for the garden.

20'

20'

- Hardy and tough
- Silvery green leaves
- Fragrant late spring flowers
- Growth rate: medium to fast; 12 to 15 inches per year
- Zones 3 to 7

Native from southern Europe to central Asia. Its hardiness and fast growth rate make it useful as a windbreak. Reaches 20 feet.

USES: Though less useful for home landscape design than other choices, it holds its leaves relatively close to the ground and provides a fast-growing windbreak. The silvery leaves also blend well with other garden colors. In addition, it has value as a bird refuge, offering shelter and small fruits.

SITING AND CARE: Plant it in full sun. Tolerant of dry and high pH soils. Canker diseases can shorten the life expectancy considerably, especially in zones 5 to 7. Best in coldest zones.

RELATED SPECIES: *Eleagnus pungens* (thorny elaeagnus) is an evergreen shrub from Japan, with silvery foliage, useful in zones 7 to 9. Forms a mound 3 to 6 feet high and wider than it is tall. Selected cultivars have variegated foliage and a neater habit.

EUCALYPTUS

yoo-kuh-LIP-tuss

Gum tree

35'

20'

- Tough and adaptable, well suited to low-maintenance regimes
- Showy bark, some have showy flowers
- Growth rate: fast, 2 to 3 feet per year
- Zones 9 to 10 (in the West)

A strong, vigorous grower, gums are impressive trees that can anchor a landscape. Native to Australia and adapted to California and Arizona. Most of the gums will reach 50 to 70 feet.

USES: Good shade or windbreak tree that can double as a privacy screen or specimen.

SITING AND CARE: Place it where fast shade is required, where tree has room to grow, and where fallen leaf and stem debris won't cause a problem. Avoid pruning from spring to fall to discourage Eucalyptus longhorn beetle infestation. Even though eucalyptus species are listed as hardy in zones 9 and 10, this does not apply to those zones in the Southeast, where climatic extremes and humidity hamper their success.

RECOMMENDED SPECIES: Over 60 species are in cultivation. *E. cinerea* (Argyle apple) grows to 50 feet tall, with reddish bark, graying on older trees. Juvenile leaves are silvery blue and disklike, and persist on older trees. 'Pendula' is weeping, with silver leaves. *E. citriodora* (lemon-scented gum) grows very tall (70 feet) in time, with powdery white, pink, or gray bark. Adult leaves are lemon-scented when crushed. *E. ficifolia* (red-flowering gum) is a medium-sized (to 25 feet), rapid-growing tree that does well in coastal regions. When in full flower, its usually bright red blossoms are attractive against its dark green canopy of large, heavy leaves. The foliage hides most of the branches from view.

Lemon gum (E. citriodora)

Silver mountain gum (E. pulverulenta)

Red-flowering gum (E. ficifolia)

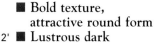

ERIOBOTRYA JAPONICA

air-ee-oh-BOH-tree-uh
ja-PON-ih-kuh

Loquat

- Bold texture, attractive round form
- Lustrous dark evergreen leaves
- Delicious fruit ripens by early summer
- Growth rate: medium, 10 to 15 feet per year
- Zones 8 to 10

Loquat is a medium-size ornamental tree with the bonus of edible fruit. Native to China and Japan. With age it grows 30 feet tall and wide.

USES: Fits nicely in many areas—shrub borders, wall espalier, and patio gardens. Loquat is versatile; use it for coarse textural contrast in the landscape.

SITING AND CARE: Exhibits good drought tolerance; but when the tree is fruiting, water regularly. Prune carefully to avoid fire blight, a serious problem.

RECOMMENDED VARIETIES AND RELATED SPECIES: 'Gold Nugget' bears large, yellow-orange fruit. 'MacBeth' has very large fruit with a yellow skin and creamy flesh. 'Champagne' has yellow-skinned, white-fleshed fruit, juicy and tart.

The rounded form of loquat shows off its coarse tropical foliage and small golden fruit.

E. globulus (blue gum) is potentially a very large tree but is excessively fast growing, weak wooded, and is likely to be seriously damaged by occasional freezes in zones 8 and 9. The selection 'Compacta' is very dense and more useful than the species. Several subspecies are known.

E. gunnii (cider gum) is a large tree, at least 70 feet tall in time, with bicolored pale green-and-white bark. Juvenile leaves are nearly circular and fused in pairs. Yellow flowers are showy in early autumn.

E. pauciflora subsp. *niphophila* (snow gum) is a small, slow-growing, wide-spreading, open tree that reaches 20 to 25 feet. The trunk often turns and bends, creating an interesting effect. Silvery blue, spear-shaped foliage contrasts gracefully with its peeling bark. Wind tolerant, it is useful in open spaces or on slopes.

E. polyanthemos (silver dollar gum) is a medium-size (45 to 50 feet), fast-growing tree with a slender, interesting, upright growth habit. The trunk can be multistemmed or single-trunked. Mottled, flaking bark adds to its visual and textural appeal. The younger leaves of this tree are quite novel—rounded and suspended individually on light twigs, they look like silver dollars. A hardy and tolerant tree, it struggles in wet or poorly drained places but thrives in coastal or dry conditions.

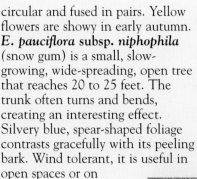

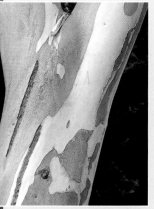

Snow gum (E. pauciflora var. niphophila)

Argyle apple (E. cinerea)

Cider gum (E. gunnii)

FAGUS SYLVATICA

FAY-guss sill-VAH-tih-kuh

European beech

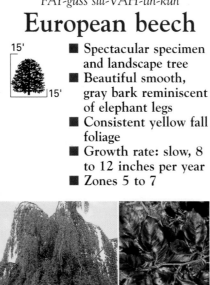

- Spectacular specimen and landscape tree
- Beautiful smooth, gray bark reminiscent of elephant legs
- Consistent yellow fall foliage
- Growth rate: slow, 8 to 12 inches per year
- Zones 5 to 7

'Pendula' (above) offers a graceful form, while 'Tricolor' (above right) offers splendid foliage color.

A large and stately tree highly valued for its smooth gray bark and glossy green leaves, which turn a yellow-bronze in autumn. Will reach 70 feet tall and 60 feet wide. **USES:** Great specimen or accent for large backyards or open areas and for framing. A tree for posterity. **SITING AND CARE:** Best in full sun, will tolerate light shade. Adapts to many soils. Allow it plenty of room and mulch widely around it; branches tend to flow to the ground.

RECOMMENDED VARIETIES AND RELATED SPECIES: 'Asplenifolia' has fernlike dark green foliage. 'Pendula' has strongly weeping branches. 'Riversii' has purple foliage from early spring through summer, purple-green in fall. *Fagus grandifolia* (American beech) is also large; use in open spaces. Dark green summer leaves change to golden bronze in fall. The leaves stay on the tree for a long time afterwards. Silver-gray bark is enhanced by its rugged structure and wide crown. Zones 4 to 8.

In fall, the Franklin tree really shines when the delicate flowers open and the foliage reddens.

FRANKLINIA ALATAMAHA

frank-LIN-ee-uh al-ah-TAH-mah-ha

Franklin tree

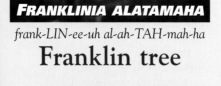

- Flowers late summer into fall
- Lustrous leaves are bright green, turning mahogany red in fall
- Growth rate: slow to moderate, 6 to 8 inches per year
- Zones 6 to 8

With white flowers resembling single camellias in late summer and fall, Franklin tree can accent a patio or courtyard well. Once native to the lowlands of Georgia, it is now extinct in the wild. Discovered by John Bartram of Philadelphia and named for his friend, Benjamin Franklin. With age, it grows 20 to 30 feet tall.

USES: A good choice for the large landscape bed. Place it to show off its attractive white flowers. Use as background, and contrast it with small blooming shrubs, such as viburnums, spirea, and azaleas.

SITING AND CARE: Requires moist, acid soils. Best in full sun, but tolerates partial shade. Susceptible to verticillium wilt.

FRAXINUS AMERICANA

FRAK-sih-nuss uh-mare-ih-CAN-uh

White ash

25'
15'

- Sturdy shade tree, lovely spreading form
- Outstanding red-purple fall foliage
- Growth rate: medium, 12 to 16 inches per year
- Zones 4 to 9

White ash is a bright looking, prized ornamental shade tree for residential landscapes. Native to southern Canada, south to Florida and Texas. In maturity it develops a majestic spreading structure 80 to 100 feet tall and about 40 feet wide.

USES: Locate it at the southwest corner of the house for shade or in the backyard. Makes an excellent street tree.

SITING AND CARE: Plant in full sun and prune only to retain natural shape. Tolerant of a wide variety of soil and site conditions. Seed-bearing samaras (similar to those of maples) cause a litter and weed problem. Use seedless cultivars.

RECOMMENDED VARIETIES: 'Autumn Applause', 'Autumn Purple', and 'Rose Hill' are all cultivars that were selected for their deep green leaves, which reliably turn reddish purple in fall, as well as for being seedless.

The white ash cultivar 'Autumn Purple' combines a very usable garden form with reliable fall color.

FRAXINUS PENNSYLVANICA

FRAK-sih-nuss pen-sill-VAN-ih-kuh

Green ash

20'
15'

- Upright, broadly pyramidal, medium-sized tree
- Leaves are bright green in summer, yellow-gold in fall in most years
- Drought-tolerant tree
- Growth rate: medium to fast, 12 to 18 inches per year
- Zones 3 to 9

Excellent shade tree, adaptable to many soil types, green ash is native from southern Canada south to Florida and Texas. Will grow to about 60 feet tall and 30 feet wide.

USES: Great for framing, shade, and in backyard corner plantings. It is commonly planted in the front yard of residential landscapes and for shade, south and west of houses and patios. It's a good street tree.

SITING AND CARE: Grows best in moist, well-drained soils, but also tolerates dry, compacted soils. Seed litter can be very heavy, so use seedless cultivars (see below).

RECOMMENDED VARIETIES: 'Marshall's Seedless' is the oldest nonfruiting cultivar and still among the very best. 'Patmore' is upright with an oval crown; a hardy specimen with good summer foliage color. 'Summit' has an upright, pyramidal form with a strong central leader and yellow fall color.

When mature, a large green ash in full fall color makes a grand statement in any landscape.

With consistent, lovely fall color and unique fan-shaped leaves, Ginkgo is not quite like any other tree.

GINKGO BILOBA

GING-koh bye-LOH-buh

Ginkgo

20'
10'

- Pyramidal when young; broad and spreading with age
- Leaves turn bright yellow in fall
- Growth rate: slow to medium, 8 to 12 inches per year
- Zones 4 to 8

Ginkgo is a large, unique tree native to eastern China. Grows to 75 feet tall and 50 feet wide.

USES: Use as a shade or specimen tree in large yards or estates. Male clones are excellent street trees.
SITING AND CARE: Plant in full sun with plenty of room to grow; it becomes somewhat spreading with age. Be sure to select a male clone to avoid messy, smelly fruit. Free of insects and disease. Prune only to remove broken branches.
RECOMMENDED VARIETIES: 'Autumn Gold' has a handsome and symmetrical form and reaches 50 feet. It is nonfruiting and has excellent fall color. 'Fastigiata' and 'Princeton Sentry'® are narrow forms and are also male clones. 'Saratoga' is oval in shape.

GLEDITSIA TRIACANTHOS VAR. INERMIS

gleh-DIT-see-uh try-uh-CAN-thuss

Thornless honey locust

Casting only a dappled shade, thornless honeylocusts are popular street trees.

25'
20'

- Leaves and branches provide wonderful fine texture and dappled shade
- Branches and slightly open habit allow turf growth underneath the canopy
- Growth rate: medium to fast, 16 to 18 inches per year
- Zones 3 to 9

With its graceful, refined form and distinctive compound leaves, honey locust adds textural diversity. Native to the central U. S., east to Pennsylvania. It can grow 100 feet tall and 50 feet wide.

USES: Use it for filtered or dappled shade over a deck or patio, or near a shady perennial garden.
SITING AND CARE: Adapts to a wide range of soils. Mimosa webworm is a serious problem in some regions and in some years. Leathery seedpods are a major litter problem around streets and yards. Use nonfruiting cultivars.
RECOMMENDED VARIETIES: 'Moraine' is the oldest and one of the best cultivars, with vase-shaped form and the greatest resistance to mimosa webworm. 'Skyline' is upright and pyramidal with golden fall color. 'Halka' is vigorous with pendulous branches and few fruits. Sunburst® has yellow spring foliage.

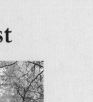

Great for a woodland setting, Carolina silverbell's open structure shows off its blooms.

HALESIA TETRAPTERA

hah-LEE-zee-uh teh-trup-TARE-uh

Carolina silverbell

12'
12'

- Clusters of white, bell-shaped flowers in late spring
- Small to medium size
- Pyramidal in youth; rounded with age
- Growth rate: medium to slow, 8 to 10 inches per year
- Zones 5 to 8

Flowers develop into four-winged fruits that remain attractive in winter. Native to southeastern U. S. With age, it reaches 20 to 30 feet tall.

USES: Place it near a patio or landscape bed where flowers can be seen easily. Also a good addition to shrub and woodland borders and in groupings with other plants, especially evergreens.
SITING AND CARE: Site in full sun or in partial shade as an understory or woodland tree. Can become chlorotic in high pH soils.
RELATED SPECIES: *Halesia monticola* (mountain silverbell) is a larger version of *H. tetraptera*, to 60 feet tall and wide, with larger flowers and fruits. It is slightly more cold hardy than *H. tetraptera*.

ILEX OPACA

EYE-lex oh-PAH-kuh

American holly

12'
8'

- Evergreen, short-spined leaves
- Handsome red berries on female plants
- Good for background color and massing
- Growth rate: slow, 5 to 7 inches per year
- Zones 6 to 9

Native to the East, from New England to north Florida and west to Missouri and Texas, American holly has dozens of cultivars.

Mature trees can reach up to 45 feet tall.

USES: Upright pyramidal shape and dense foliage texture make a nice contrast to light-colored and looser plants. Slow growth suits it for small gardens.

SITING AND CARE: Protect from winter winds. Plant one male to several females to assure fruit set.

RECOMMENDED VARIETIES AND RELATED SPECIES: 'Merry Christmas' has dark leaves and is fast growing. 'Greenleaf' has strong pyramidal form and bright red fruit. 'Croonenburg' is compact with heavy fruit set. *Ilex × attenuata* 'Fosterii' has narrowly pyramidal form and is useful in zones 7 to 9.

A consistently pleasing blend of green leaves and red berries makes American holly a favorite.

JUGLANS NIGRA

JUG-lans NYE-gruh

Black walnut

25'
20'

- Large tree with somewhat open crown
- Attractive bark adds texture and color
- Nice shade tree for parklike sites
- Growth rate: medium, 12 to 15 inches per year
- Zones 5 to 9

Walnut wood has long been prized for furniture; its nuts are edible (and

beloved by squirrels). Native to eastern and central United States. It commonly reaches 50 feet, and can grow up to 100 feet tall with age.

USES: A good tree to use on larger lots and acreages but it is too large for most residential landscapes. Some other plants won't grow in areas near walnut due to juglone, a root exudate that walnut produces.

SITING AND CARE: Allow this tree room to grow. Eliminate grass competition near the tree and mulch around the base.

Black walnut is at its showiest when the leaves turn color and contrast with its rugged dark bark.

JUNIPERUS VIRGINIANA

joo-NIH-per-us ver-jih-nee-AYE-nuh

Eastern red cedar

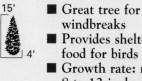

15'
4'

- Great tree for windbreaks
- Provides shelter and food for birds
- Growth rate: medium, 8 to 12 inches per year
- Zones 3 to 9

Although its cultivars may be more attractive than the species, eastern red cedar is a good utility tree and is native to large areas east of the Rocky Mountains. Can grow to

60 feet tall and 15 to 20 feet wide with great age.

USES: Holds its dense foliage low to the ground, which is useful for screening. Somewhat coarse for the urban landscape, but the cultivars can be good screening plants.

SITING AND CARE: Susceptible to mites and bagworms.

RECOMMENDED VARIETIES: 'Manhattan Blue' has a compact, pyramidal form and bluish green foliage. 'Glauca' is narrow and loosely pyramidal, to 25 feet tall, with silver-blue foliage. 'Canaertii' has a compact pyramidal form, dark green tufted foliage, and grows 25 to 30 feet tall.

With low-growing limbs, a textured trunk, and fine foliage, a mature eastern red cedar is a noble tree.

Both flowers and seed-pods are fine features of the golden rain tree.

KOELREUTERIA PANICULATA

kohl-roo-TEER-ee-uh pan-ick-yoo-LAY-tuh

Golden rain tree

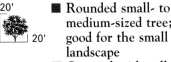

20'
20'

- Rounded small- to medium-sized tree; good for the small landscape
- Covered with yellow flowers in midsummer
- Attractive papery capsules in fall
- Growth rate: medium, 8 to 12 inches per year
- Zones 5 to 9

Golden rain tree is an outstanding, low-input, high-output tree. Native to China and Korea. Reaches 35 feet tall and wide at maturity.

USES: There are few other good trees with yellow flowers in summer. Locate it for shade on the southwest side of a patio or home. This is a great tree for the urban landscape in less-than-perfect soils.

SITING AND CARE: Tolerates cold, heat, drought, and low fertility. Requires no special care, other than to water during extended periods of drought.

RECOMMENDED VARIETIES: 'September' flowers four to six weeks later than the species.

LABURNUM X WATERERI

lah-BURR-num WAH-ter-er-eye

Golden chain tree

A good tree for most landscapes, golden chain tree enchants with its hanging golden flowers.

15'
6'

- Large shrub or small tree; good for the small landscape
- Hanging chains of yellow flowers in spring
- Growth rate: medium, 8 to 12 inches per year
- Zones 6 to 8

A useful tree for the small, urban landscape, golden chain tree grows best in eastern and western coast areas. It is not a plant for the Deep South. Can grow 20 to 30 feet tall.

USES: Place at corners of a house for softening or as a single specimen in a lawn. Best incorporated into a landscape bed, in a shrub border or in masses, or for vivid spring color

and neutral background the rest of the year.

SITING AND CARE: Needs light shade in the afternoon. Prune each year to train into a tree by removing basal suckers and low-hanging branches. Twig blight can become a serious problem; sanitation and pruning will minimize it.

RECOMMENDED VARIETIES AND RELATED SPECIES: 'Vossii' has a dense growth habit with large chains of flowers up to 2 feet long. *L. alpinum* (Scotch laburnum), one of the parents of this hybrid, is slightly more cold hardy but not widely available.

LAGERSTROEMIA INDICA

lah-ger-STREE-mee-uh IN-dih-kuh

Crape myrtle

15'
15'

- Slow-growing, multitrunked, small tree
- Profuse late summer flowers in brilliant colors
- Excellent fall color
- Handsome multicolored bark
- Growth rate: slow to medium, 6 to 10 inches per year
- Zones 7 to 9

A good small tree with many uses for the South and West, common crape myrtle is native to China and Korea. Eventually reaches 20 to 30 feet tall and wide.

USES: Underplanted with a low ground cover, this tree makes a handsome specimen with superb trunk and bark interest year-round in hot, sunny southern gardens.

SITING AND CARE: Plant in full sun. Feed occasionally to keep foliage healthy. Prune when dormant to produce larger flowers.

RECOMMENDED VARIETIES: Many cultivars are available. 'Comanche' has deep hot-pink flowers and dark glossy green foliage, and is mildew resistant. 'Natchez' has dark, cinnamon-colored, peeling bark, dark green leaves, white flowers. 'Biloxi' is upright, multistemmed, with light bronze leaves, pale pink flowers.

An underappreciated feature of crape myrtle, the trunks and bark offer interest year-round.

LARIX KAEMPFERI

LARE-icks KAM-fur-eye

Japanese larch

20' / 15'

- Large, stately habit
- Soft-textured foliage is chartreuse in spring, blue-green in summer; golden yellow in fall
- Evergreen look on a deciduous tree
- Growth rate: medium to fast, 12 to 15 inches per year
- Zones 4 to 7

The delicate blue-green foliage of Japanese larch turns golden yellow in fall. Native to Japan. Can grow to 75 feet tall and 40 feet wide.

USES: With its massive, horizontal branches, this is a great choice for a specimen tree, for framing, or for the corner of a large residential backyard. It is worth growing for its color and texture alone. It also works well as a background plant along with or behind small- or medium-sized flowering shrubs.

SITING AND CARE: Plant it in a well-drained, open location. Best in cool, moist soils; tolerates wet soils.

RECOMMENDED VARIETIES AND RELATED SPECIES: *L. decidua* (European larch) has an even more graceful form than the Japanese genus.

Larix decidua 'Pendula' (above right) is a curious weeping form of Japanese larch (above).

LIQUIDAMBAR STYRACIFLUA

lih-kwih-DAM-bar sty-ruh-SIH-flu-uh

Sweet gum

20' / 12'

- Bright green, glossy, star-shaped leaves turn crimson to purple in fall
- Golfball-size, spiny fruit can be messy
- Growth rate: medium to fast, 12 to 15 inches per year
- Zones 5 to 10

Multicolored foliage in the fall has made this tree a favorite. Native to the eastern United States. Can grow to 75 feet tall and 50 feet wide.

USES: Urban shade or street tree.

SITING AND CARE: Best in moist, rich soils. Needs room, both to spread and also for root development. Spikey "gum ball" litter over a long season can be annoying underfoot. Not reliable in colder areas of zone 5.

RECOMMENDED VARIETIES: 'Burgundy' leaves turn wine-red to deep purple in fall. 'Festival' is narrow, columnar; its foliage turns yellow to peach to orange. 'Moraine' is unusually vigorous and cold hardy. 'Rotundiloba' has rounded leaf lobes, purple fall color, no fruits.

The leaves of sweet gum 'Burgundy' consistently turn a dramatic deep red in the fall.

LIRIODENDRON TULIPIFERA

leer-ee-oh-DEN-dron too-li-PIH-fur-uh

Tulip tree

30' / 15'

- Tall, broadly oval to round with age
- Unique, tulip-shaped, yellow-orange flowers
- Bright yellow fall foliage
- Growth rate: medium to fast, 15 to 18 inches per year
- Zones 5 to 9

Attractive flowers hidden in a green canopy of unusual leaves are the secret to this tree's beauty. Popular because of its quick growth, attractive form, and unique flowers. The tallest deciduous tree in North America; native to the eastern U. S. Grows 100 feet tall with age.

USES: Use in groupings with other large trees on an estate or in a large landscape for screening or massing.

SITING AND CARE: Surround it with other large trees to prevent sunscald and scorch. Inspect regularly for aphids and control when their numbers are high.

RECOMMENDED VARIETIES: 'Arnold' ('Fastigiatum') is a narrowly columnar cultivar.

The unusual flowers of the tulip tree are delightful when viewed up close.

MAGNOLIA GRANDIFLORA

mag-NOH-lee-uh grand-ih-FLOR-uh

Southern magnolia

25'
20'

- Large, glossy, dark evergreen leaves
- Large (8- to 12-inch), waxy, creamy white, very fragrant flowers late spring through summer
- Growth rate: medium, 12 to 15 inches per year depending on culture
- Zones 7 to 9

With its tropical-looking leaves, dramatic flowers, and large size, this is a tree to use as a bold statement. Grows to 65 feet and higher.

USES:. Use in massing for color (deep green foliage in winter; white flowers in summer) on large estates or residential lots. Give it room to grow; it's not for the small urban landscape.

SITING AND CARE: Locate in full sun or partial shade; protect from winter winds in the north part of the growing region.

RECOMMENDED VARIETIES: 'Edith Bogue' grows in a tight pyramidal form with narrow, lustrous, dark green leaves, and is unusually cold hardy (reportedly hardy to southern zone 5). 'Glen St. Mary' has a compact, bushy pyramidal form, 20 feet by 20 feet with lustrous, dark green leaves. 'Little Gem' is a small, dense, shrubby specimen with small leaves.

Southern magnolia does everything on a grand scale—grand flowers, grand leaves, grand fruit.

Although its classic blooms are attractive, bigleaf magnolia is more often grown for its tropical foliage.

MAGNOLIA MACROPHYLLA

mag-NOH-lee-uh mack-roh-FYE-luh

Bigleaf magnolia

25'
15'

- Huge leaves, from 24 to 36 inches long
- White, fragrant flowers, 8 to 12 inches across, develop large, rose-colored fruits
- Round-headed, medium-sized tree
- Growth rate: slow to medium
- Zones 5 to 9

Bigleaf magnolia will give a luxuriant tropical look to the cold-winter landscape. Its leaves are among the largest on a nontropical tree and are its main distinction. Native to the Deep South and to Kentucky and West Virginia. Will reach 35 to 40 feet.

USES: Best as a specimen or novelty due to its large leaves and fruit. Its striking foliage combines well with other colors and textures in the landscape; could be the centerpiece of a tropically themed garden.

SITING AND CARE: Protect from wind, which will tear the huge leaves apart. Like most magnolias, will take considerable shade.

MAGNOLIA X SOULANGIANA

mag-NOH-lee-uh soo-lan-gee-AN-uh

Saucer magnolia

15'
15'

- Pink and purple flowers in spring
- Open, spreading form
- Small- to medium-sized tree
- Growth rate: medium, 10 to 12 inches per year
- Zones 5 to 9

A medium-sized tree with great shape and form; blooms heavily even when it's young—often when only 4 feet tall. Native to China. Reaches 20 to 30 feet tall.

USES: Its statuesque form and bold foliage texture all season are attractive, but floral display is the prime reason for using this tree.

SITING AND CARE: Plant on the north or east side of the property to delay growth until spring frosts are over. Frost damage generally occurs in 1 out of 4 years.

RECOMMENDED VARIETIES AND RELATED SPECIES: 'Alexandrina' has early-blooming, rose-purple and white flowers. 'Brozzonii,' a later flowering cultivar, has white flowers up to 10 inches across. 'Rustica Rubra' has red-purple flowers, whitened inside.

The flowers of 'Alexandra' (top) and 'Elizabeth' (right) are stunning up close.

MAGNOLIA STELLATA

mag-NOH-lee-uh steh-LAH-tah

Star magnolia

10'
10'

- Many-petaled, 4-inch, white spring flowers before leaves
- Broadly oval small tree or large shrub
- Growth rate: slow to medium, 6 to 8 inches per year
- Zones 5 to 9

A small tree with a shrubby form, this magnolia has many uses in the landscape. Native to Japan. Will reach about 20 feet tall and wide.

USES: A good plant for an entryway border, surrounded with perennials and ground cover, or as an accent in the small residential landscape.

SITING AND CARE: Locate it in full sun. Water in dry periods. It naturally retains a tight dense form without pruning.

RECOMMENDED VARIETIES AND RELATED SPECIES: 'Royal Star' bears pink buds opening to white flowers. 'Waterlily' is later flowering than the species and highly fragrant. M. × *loebneri* (Loebner magnolia) is a hybrid between M. *stellata* and M. *kobus*. The original selection was 'Merrill', a fine medium-sized tree.

Star magnolia's straplike, star-shaped flowers burst into bloom with the daffodils and narcissus of early spring.

MAGNOLIA VIRGINIANA

mag-NOH-lee-ah ver-jih-nee-AYE-na

Sweet bay magnolia

20'
15'

- Sweet-scented, 2- to 3-inch flowers; never overpowering
- Branches tossing in the wind expose the silvery undersides of the deciduous to semievergreen leaves
- Growth rate: medium to fast, 10 to 15 inches per year
- Zones 5 to 9

A good shrubby tree for wet areas of the landscape, sweet bay magnolia is native to coastal regions from Massachusetts to Florida. In the Deep South it can be evergreen. Variable size: in the North, 10 to 20 feet; in the South, 30 to 50 feet.

USES: A good smaller version of southern magnolia (deciduous north of zone 7), it can be grown in the shrub border.

SITING AND CARE: Tolerates semishady conditions and moist to occasionally wet soils. The best magnolia for seashore conditions.

Fragrant flowers and attractive form make sweet bay magnolia ideal for the intimate garden.

MALUS HYBRIDS

MAWL-us

Crabapple

15'   15'

- Spectacular spring flowers
- Small, bright red fruits are favored by birds, and remain well into fall
- Growth rate: slow growing
- Zones 4 to 8

A good-looking tree with long, slender, weeping branches, its small size makes it very usable in the urban landscape. Grows well in temperate regions of the U.S.

USES: Its asymmetrical form contrasts well in the perennial garden and is in scale with most spring bulbs, such as late-blooming daffodils and tulips.

SITING AND CARE: Locate it in full sun for best flowering. Keep the structure of the tree slightly open for good air circulation and disease resistance. Fire blight, apple scab, and powdery mildew can be problems; select resistant varieties.

RECOMMENDED VARIETIES AND RELATED SPECIES: Hundreds of cultivars of several species and hybrids are available, a few of which are listed below.

Crabapple 'Golden Hornet' in fruit

Crabapple 'Red Splendor' in fruit

Crabapple 'Dolgo'

Japanese flowering crabapple (Malus floribunda), above, and Crabapple 'David', left

Crabapple 'Dorothea'

CRABAPPLE CULTIVARS

Name	Fruit	Flower	Other
'Bob White'	Yellow, gold	White	Excellent floral display, may not be consistent from year to year
'David'	Scarlet	Snow white	Attractive round form, sparse flowers
'Donald Wyman'	Red	White	Effective winter fruit display, good rounded form, attractive peeling bark
'Indian Magic'	Red-orange	Pink	Apricot-orange fall foliage, attractive bark, excellent fruit display
'Liset'	Maroon, red	Rose red	Peach-colored fall foliage, attractive fall fruit display
'Mary Potter'	Red	White	Attractive spreading form, attractive bark
'Molten Lava'	Red-orange	White	Spreading, weeping form, good structure in winter
'Roy Ormiston'	Orange-yellow	White	Deep furrowed orange-colored bark. Attractive fruit in fall
'Prairiefire'	Purple-red	Coral red	Red-tinged foliage, orange fall foliage
'Professor Sprenger'	Orange-red	White	Good persistent fruits
'Red Jade'	Red	White to pink	Spreading, weeping form, very popular
M. *sargentii*	Red	White	Graceful, horizontal, spreading form to 9 feet high, 15 feet wide.
'Sugar Tyme'	Red	White	Good form and fruit, best for the South
M. × *zumi* 'Calocarpa'	Red	White	Excellent flowers, abundant tiny red fruit

METASEQUOIA GLYPTOSTROBOIDES

*meh-tuh-seh-KWOY-yuh
glip-toh-stroh-BOY-deez*

Dawn redwood

25'

12'

- Bright-green foliage turns russet-orange and drops in fall
- Magnificent pyramidal form creates effect of a prehistoric forest
- Deep-fluted bark and buttressed trunk
- Growth rate: fast, about 2 feet per year
- Zones 5 to 8

Dawn redwood is a fine-textured, fast-growing tree when sited correctly. Native to central China. Grows to 80 feet or more.
USES: A great tree for the corner of a large residential lot. Combine it with large shrubs or small trees for screening, or wherever there is ample space.
SITING AND CARE: Best in moist or even wet soil, in sun or shade.
RECOMMENDED VARIETIES: 'National' and 'Sheridan Spire' have narrow, upright growth habits.

Dawn redwood's attractively colored and textured bark combines well with many other garden textures.

NYSSA SYLVATICA

NISS-uh sil-VAT-tih-kuh

Black gum or sour gum

20'

15'

- Dark, glossy leaves turn crimson in fall
- Pyramidal structure like pin oak when young
- Horizontal, twisting branches
- Medium-size tree
- Growth rate: slow to medium, 8 to 12 inches per year
- Zones 5 to 9

With strong fall color and a distinctive pyramidal structure, black gum can become a dramatic tree. It can reach 40 to 75 feet tall and 20 to 45 feet wide.
USES: This is a good specimen tree, but you can also use it as a background plant.
SITING AND CARE: Can be slow getting started, especially in poor or dry soil. Prefers moist, well-drained, acid soils and a bit of wind protection. Good on elevated pond or stream banks. Juicy, purple-black fruit can be messy over paving.

A good medium-size tree for the landscape, black gum stands out for its glossy-textured fall foliage.

OLEA EUROPAEA

OH-lee-uh yoor-roh-PEE-uh

Olive

15'

15'

- Attractive gnarly grey trunk and form
- Gray-green willowlike leaves
- A moderate-size tree with edible fruit
- Growth rate: slow, 10 to 12 inches per year with irrigation
- Zones 9 to 10

Easy to transplant and relocate even in old age, the olive is native to the Mediterranean region and grows

well in Arizona and California. It reaches 25 to 30 feet tall and wide.
USES: Grow in small landscapes, locating it where fruit droppage is not a problem. Adapts well to hot, dry summers and coastal regions.
SITING AND CARE: Plant in full sun and well-drained soil. Fruit stains paving. Pollen causes serious allergic reactions in some people; before planting it, check to see if it is banned in your area.
RECOMMENDED VARIETIES: 'Manzanillo' is a commercial grove olive with a spreading habit. 'Little Ollie' is a dense, shrubby tree (to 12 feet), useful as a hedge. 'Wilsoni' has a spreading habit to 25 feet and produces few or no fruit.

With a gnarly trunk and gray leaves, olive offers gardeners a taste of the Mediterranean.

A strong native tree, sourwood's upright form is often decorated with red fall foliage and hanging ivory seedpods at the same time. It's also one of the earliest trees to color in the fall.

OXYDENDRUM ARBOREUM

awk-sih-DEN-drum ar-BORE-ee-um

Sourwood

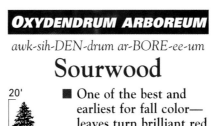

20'
15'

- One of the best and earliest for fall color—leaves turn brilliant red
- A tree for all seasons
- White flowers in midsummer, followed by white fruits like strings of pearls in the fall
- Growth rate: medium, 12 to 15 inches per year
- Zones 5 to 9

Second only to flowering dogwood in small native-tree appeal, sourwood is an excellent tree for small spaces, with multiseason appeal and an upright form. Native to the eastern United States. It will eventually reach 50 to 75 feet tall in good sites.

USES: Use it as an accent plant to soften harsh corners, making sure to plant it where its year-round appeal can be seen. Grow it on the edge of decks, by the patio or terrace. It can also be used as a specimen.

SITING AND CARE: Performs best in acidic, well-drained soil. Tolerates moderate drought but is not very competitive. Avoid cultivating around root zone.

With its huge leaves and exotic purple flowers, empress tree is a good choice for a tropical flair.

PAULOWNIA TOMENTOSA

paw-LOH-nee-uh toh-men-TOH-suh

Empress tree

30'
30'

- Large leaves and flowers impart a tropical, bold texture
- Showy, violet flowers in midspring
- Growth rate: fast, normally 2 feet per year, but can be more in a good year
- Zones 7 to 9 (and southern zone 6)

An interesting tree with an unusual shape and look, empress tree lends a tropical effect to the landscape. Native to China; naturalized in parts of the southeastern U. S. Grows to 50 feet tall and wide.

USES: Plant it near other trees and shrubs, keeping its eventual spread in mind. Good for fast growth and green foliage. Can be weedy.

SITING AND CARE: Grow in full sun or partial shade. Prune only to remove deadwood. In zone 6 it will occasionally be killed back in winter. The spectacular flowers form on two-year-old wood, so limit pruning to late spring. This is a soft-wooded tree, often killed back to the ground annually in the North.

Amur cork tree is named for its fissured bark. It is a handsome yet rugged, very adaptable tree.

PHELLODENDRON AMURENSE

feh-loh-DEN-dron ah-mer-EN-see

Amur cork tree

15'
15'

- Picturesque, open habit with maturity
- Deep-fissured gnarly bark
- Grows well in difficult sites
- Growth rate: slow to medium, 6 to 10 inches per year
- Zones 3 to 7

Amur cork tree is a tough tree of medium size with a handsomely

rugged trunk and wide-spreading limbs and corky bark. Native to China and Japan. It can reach up to 30 to 50 feet tall with an equal or wider spread.

USES: Use it in corner plantings or along paths for close-up views of the bark. A good hardy tree for creating dappled shade.

SITING AND CARE: Adapts to many soil types. Fruit on female trees is more a liability than an asset, as it litters and stains walks.

RECOMMENDED VARIETIES: 'Macho®' and 'Shademaster®' are male selections with good pest resistance, dark green leaves, and a moderately spreading growth habit.

PICEA ABIES

pye-SEE-uh AY-beez

Norway spruce

25'

15'

- Strong upright form
- Evergreen foliage on pendulous branches
- Growth rate: medium, 12 to 18 inches per year
- Zones 3 to 8

A graceful, upright tree, Norway spruce is native to northern and central Europe. It can reach over 100 feet tall.

USES: Plant it on estates, acreages or large residential lots for wind screens, boundary markers, or background. With space, it makes a good landscape specimen.

SITING AND CARE: Does well in cool, moist conditions but tolerates drought in the central Midwest. Inspect for mites.

RECOMMENDED VARIETIES AND RELATED SPECIES: 'Pumila' is a dwarf (to 4 feet), globular tree with dense, compact needles and branches. 'Nidiformis' (bird's-nest spruce) is a dwarf, dense plant with a spreading habit that often has a slight depression in the top, hence its name.

Norway spruce has an upright form with slightly drooping branches.

PICEA ORIENTALIS

pye-SEE-uh oh-ree-en-TALE-iss

Oriental spruce

12'

8'

- Graceful, drooping habit
- Dense, deep, glossy green foliage
- Tolerates hot, dry summers better than other spruces
- Growth rate: slow, 8 to 10 inches per year
- Zones 6 to 8 (and milder areas of zone 5)

Its graceful form, glossy dark green foliage, and heat tolerance make Oriental spruce one of the finest landscape conifers. Native to Asia Minor. With age, will reach up to 80 feet tall.

USES: Use it as a specimen tree in a medium-sized shrub border or let it perform as a screen.

SITING AND CARE: Adapts to poor infertile soils. Protect from cold winter winds.

RECOMMENDED VARIETIES: 'Aurea' is a selection with golden yellow emerging foliage. 'Gowdy' has a narrow, columnar form with rich green needles and grows to 10 feet. 'Skylands' is a striking selection with golden foliage, growing slowly at first but eventually becoming a large tree.

A good all-around conifer, Oriental spruce grows slowly into a large tree and tolerates hot, dry weather.

PICEA PUNGENS GLAUCA

pye-SEE-uh oh-MOH-ree-kah

Colorado blue spruce

15'

6'

- Silvery blue needles, with numerous very blue cultivars
- Strongly pyramidal form
- Growth rate: slow, 8 to 12 inches per year
- Zones 3 to 7

This is a popular tree for cool-summer climates. Grows best in the Northeast and New England states, but adapts to the Midwest and the upper South. Native to the Rocky Mountains from the U.S. to Mexico. Will eventually grow 60 to 75 feet tall.

USES: Colorado blue spruce is grown for its blue, stiff needles; it makes an effective specimen as well as a good screen.

SITING AND CARE: Best in well-drained soil with adequate moisture. Inspect for mites and adelgids, and control if found in high numbers; they can disfigure this tree's symmetrical habit.

RECOMMENDED VARIETIES: Many cultivars are available. 'Hoopsii', 'Koster', and 'Moerheim' are three of the most popular for intense blue foliage.

Colorado blue spruce 'Koster' is one of the bluer forms of this popular tree.

PINUS DENSIFLORA

PYE-nuss den-sih-FLOR-uh

Japanese red pine

The year-round interest of Japanese red pine is in large part because of its flaking, colorful bark.

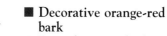

15'
15'

- Decorative orange-red bark
- Densely conical when young; open and picturesque with age
- Growth rate: slow to medium, 8 to 12 inches per year
- Zones 6 to 7 (and milder parts of zone 5)

This native of Japan and Korea can be used as a subject for bonsai and is a handsome specimen. It can reach 50 feet tall and wide.

USES: Great appeal from both bark and trunks.

SITING AND CARE: Prefers well-drained soils and sunny conditions.

Needs protection from wind. Allow needles to fall around tree and form a natural mulch.

RECOMMENDED VARIETIES AND RELATED SPECIES: 'Oculus-draconis' (dragon's eye pine) has yellow-banded needles and picturesque habit, and is slower growing. 'Pendula' is an attractive weeping form. 'Umbraculifera' (Tanyosho pine) is multiple-trunked and umbrella-shaped.

'Umbraculifera' or Tanyosho pine

PINUS NIGRA

PYE-nuss NYE-gruh

Austrian pine

18'
18'

- Dense, dark, evergreen foliage
- Tolerant of heat, drought, poor conditions and soils
- Growth rate: medium, 8 to 12 inches per year.
- Zones 4 to 7

A very adaptable tree, Austrian pine often develops interesting, rugged trunks with maturity.

Austrian pine is a tough, reliable performer in the garden, tolerating most conditions. It is native to southern Europe, from Austria to Italy and Greece. It can grow 60 feet tall and wide.

USES: Hardy and wind resistant, it makes a good windbreak or screen. Use it as an anchoring plant in a backyard border, or in mass plantings where room allows.

SITING AND CARE: Grows well in many different sites and regions of the country. Subject to tip blight, needle blight, pine moths, and other pests, some of which can do serious damage. Pest inspection is an important part of maintenance for Austrian pine.

The fissured, colorful bark of Italian stone pine is just one of the many attributes of this fine, medium-to-large tree.

PINUS PINEA

PYE-nuss pye-NEE-uh

Italian stone pine

40'
30'

- A dense sphere when young, becoming broad and flat-topped
- Edible fruit (pine nuts)
- Moderate- to large-sized, depending on site
- Growth rate: slow to moderate
- Zones 8 to 10

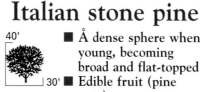

Italian stone pine starts out with a rounded shape when young but develops a broad crown with age.

These trees are very handsome when young and bring a striking air of classic Rome with age. They grow well in California valleys and northern Arizona. Native to the Mediterranean region from Turkey through southern Europe. Can reach 40 feet to 60 feet high with an equal spread.

USES: Picturesque, open, spreading shape makes this a good specimen tree. It has been used with great effect as a street tree in California. Because of its spreading habit, this is not a tree for the small garden.

SITING AND CARE: Hardy; takes heat and drought once established. An excellent choice for sandy soils and coastal gardens.

PINUS STROBUS

PYE-nuss STROH-buss

Eastern white pine

15'
15'

- Soft, fine-textured needles
- Graceful branches sweep in the wind
- Somewhat open, but gentle to the eye and to the touch
- Growth rate: fast, 12 to 15 inches per year
- Zones 3 to 8

White pine is one of the fastest-growing landscape pines. It is native from southern Canada south to Georgia and west to Iowa. Can grow to more than 100 feet tall.

USES: Good for a quick screen around a patio or for corner plantings in a mixed landscape bed. Can create groves where space allows. Makes an excellent lawn tree, and the needles can be allowed to fall and mulch around the tree.

SITING AND CARE: Fine for cold sites but needs some protection from constant wind exposure, and from road salt.

RECOMMENDED VARIETIES: 'Fastigiata' has narrower branching angles and so is not so wide. Good for a limited amount of space. 'Pendula' is a graceful pendulous form that grows to at least 10 feet in 20 years and is useful as a specimen or accent.

White pine is a consistent performer, with an open habit made more graceful by its horizontal branches.

PINUS SYLVESTRIS

PYE-nuss sil-VESS-triss

Scotch pine

25'
15'

- Classic gnarled habit and shape with age
- Reddish brown, deeply textured bark
- Growth rate: medium, 8 to 12 inches per year
- Zones 3 to 8

Commonly acquired as a live Christmas tree, Scotch pine is conducive to shearing. Hardy and wind resistant, it is native to northern Europe and Siberia and is commonly grown across North America. It will eventually grow 60 to 75 feet tall.

USES: Great for screening on the property lines of most any size landscape, it can also be grown as a specimen tree in large landscapes.

SITING AND CARE: Grows best in full sun. Adapts to a wide range of soil types. Allow needles to fall; collect them under the drip line. Susceptible to needle blights, most especially in the Midwest.

RECOMMENDED VARIETIES: 'French Blue' has bright blue-green foliage on a more uniform, compact tree. 'Watereri' has steel blue needles on a densely pyramidal tree.

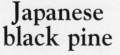

Over time, Scotch pine matures to a majestic tree with open, picturesque beauty.

PINUS THUNBERGII

PYE-nuss thun-BARE-jee-eye

Japanese black pine

15'
15'

- Large, white terminal buds
- Easily trained into picturesque shapes
- Excellent for seashore
- Growth rate: fast
- Zones 5 to 8

Japanese black pine is tolerant of a wide range of growing conditions. It is native to Japan. It can be a large tree, reaching 50 feet at maturity.

USES: Use as a stabilizer for sand dunes and seashore plantings (it is tolerant of salt spray) or as an irregular mass planting in a large landscape. Can also be used in a large border or backyard.

SITING AND CARE: Prevent drought by occasional deep watering. Prune only to retain natural shape.

RECOMMENDED VARIETIES AND RELATED SPECIES: 'Thunderhead' has heavy, dense dark green needles and a dwarf, broad habit. 'Monina' ('Majestic Beauty'®)has lustrous dark green needles and a growth habit like the species, but denser and more compactly shaped.

Popular for seaside plantings, Japanese black pine performs well in any large garden.

An underused tree, Chinese pistachio impresses many gardeners with its stunning fall color.

PISTACIA CHINENSIS

piss-TAH-shee-uh chih-NEN-siss

Chinese pistachio

15'

15'

- Bright red or orange foliage in fall
- Habit a bit gangly when young, becoming more rounded and controlled with age
- Growth rate: medium to fast, 6 to 12 inches per year (depends on moisture availability)
- Zones 7 to 9

Chinese pistachio is an overlooked but reliable tree with a good growth rate and strong fall color. Native to China. With age, it can grow to 50 feet tall and 35 feet wide.

USES: Plant it in a corner garden or use it for a patio background or street tree. Able to withstand adverse conditions, it is a good tree for urban conditions, especially drought or dry soil.

SITING AND CARE: Stake and prune when young to develop structure and a strong central leader. Once established, Chinese pistachio is a fairly low-maintenance tree, resistant to most pests and diseases.

PLATANUS X ACERIFOLIA

PLAH-tuh-nuss ah-sir-ih-FOH-lee-uh

London plane tree

35'

15'

- Gray-and-white naturally peeling bark
- Develops a wide, open outline with age
- Growth rate: medium to fast, 12 to 24 inches per year
- Zones 6 to 8, and milder parts of zone 5

Massed plantings of London plane tree create a powerful effect.

London plane tree grows well in nearly all parts of the U.S. This tree is a hybrid of *P. occidentalis* and *P. orientalis* (Oriental plane tree), a native to southeastern Europe and parts of Asia. It has the hardiness of *P. occidentalis* and the anthracnose resistance of *P. orientalis*. It can reach 100 feet tall and wide.

USES: A lovely shade tree, it is a favorite street tree and often pruned for formal effects.

SITING AND CARE: Adapts to a wide variety of soils and is resistant to anthracnose disease.

RECOMMENDED VARIETIES AND RELATED SPECIES: 'Liberty' has good resistance to powdery mildew and anthracnose. The cultivar 'Bloodgood' is rapid growing and especially resistant to anthracnose. *P. occidentalis* (sycamore) is a native tree of the eastern U. S. It is fast growing but very susceptible to anthracnose. It continually sheds twig, leaf, and branch litter, making it unsuitable for anything but a large acreage or wild area.

Yew pine is effective near a doorway or walkway when young, but it can eventually become much too large.

PODOCARPUS MACROPHYLLUS

poh-doh-CAR-pus mah-kroh-FILL-us

Yew pine

12'

3'

- Upright to oval to columnar evergreen tree or large shrub
- Four-inch-long needlelike leaves grow on slightly drooping branches
- Growth rate: slow, 6 to 10 inches per year
- Zones 8 to 10

This striking conifer has a graceful Oriental effect. Native to Japan and southern China. With age, can reach 30 feet tall and 10 feet wide.

USES: Grow as an espalier or in patio tubs and in courtyards. Also good for hedges, screens, and small gardens. Be sure to consider its mature size when planting near walks and buildings

SITING AND CARE: Grows well in full sun or partial shade; good drainage is a must.

RECOMMENDED VARIETIES: 'Maki' is a shrubby form, growing slowly to 10 feet tall. It is the form most commonly used.

POPULUS ALBA

PAH-pyoo-luss AL-buh

White poplar

30'
15'

- Columnar forms popular for fast screen and windbreak
- Dark green leaves with white undersides flutter in the wind, creating a silvery effect
- Growth rate: fast, 18 to 24 inches per year
- Whitish gray-green barks adds interest in all seasons
- Zones 4 to 9

White poplar is a good temporary tree until more reliable or long-lived trees become established. Native to Eurasia. Over time it can reach 75 feet tall and 40 feet wide. **USES:** Good for large spaces along property lines between neighboring patios and decks.
SITING AND CARE: Susceptible to many pests; limited lifespan. Prune out dead wood as it develops. Suckers freely.
RECOMMENDED VARIETIES AND RELATED SPECIES: *Populus nigra* var. *italica* (Lombardy Poplar) is useful as a very narrow screening plant, but only temporarily. It is very susceptible to cytospora canker, and grows vigorously for only a few years before succumbing. Where it thrives, it quickly grows very large. 'Pyramidalis' (bolleana poplar) is more disease resistant and durable.

When the wind catches the dark green and silver leaves of white poplar, it almost seems to shimmer.

POPULUS TREMULOIDES

PAH-pyoo-luss trem-yoo-LOY-deez

Quaking aspen

25'
8'

- Brilliant yellow fall foliage color
- Narrow and upright; good for groves
- The slightest breeze flutters the leaves
- Smooth, pale trunks and limbs
- Growth rate: fast, 12 to 18 inches per year
- Zones 2 to 6

With its leaves in constant motion, quaking aspen offers an interesting animation in the landscape. It grows best at higher elevations and in cool climates. Native from western mountains to Pennsylvania, it can reach 35 feet tall and 10 feet wide.
USES: Use for quick groves in a new landscape or in natural areas.
SITING AND CARE: Susceptible to cankers and borers. Produces many seedlings and suckers. Inspect trunk for evidence of pests.
RECOMMENDED VARIETIES AND RELATED SPECIES: *P. tremula* (European aspen) is the European equivalent of our quaking aspen; 'Erecta' is as columnar as Lombardy poplar but much more troublefree—a handsome exclamation mark in the landscape.

Justly renowned for elegant trunks and bark, quaking aspen is also impressive in fall color.

PRUNUS CERASIFERA

PROO-nuss sare-uh-SIH-fur-ah

Cherry plum or Myrobalan plum

12'
12'

- Red-purple cultivars
- White to pink flowers
- Useful, shrubby tree
- Growth rate: medium, 6 to 12 inches per year
- Zones 4 to 8

A versatile small tree, cherry plum is native to western Asia. Cultivars may be preferred over the species. Can grow to 20 feet tall and wide.

USES: Use as an anchor in the shrub border. Grows nicely in the small patio garden; scales down the size of tall brick walls and softens vertical corners.
SITING AND CARE: A full sun plant, it adapts to many soil types. Susceptible to many pests, especially cankers, aphids, caterpillars, borers, and leaf spots. Routine pest inspection is a must.
RECOMMENDED VARIETIES: 'Atropurpurea' has an upright dense form and reddish purple foliage. 'Newport' is a hardy purple-leaved selection. 'Thundercloud', another purple-leaved cultivar, bears pink flowers before the foliage.

The soft pink flowers cherry offer a good cont brightly colored bulbs of ea

PRUNUS LAUROCERASUS

PROO-nuss lah-roh-sih-RASS-suss

Cherry laurel or English laurel

When viewed up close, the blooms of cherry laurel contrast nicely with the dark, leathery leaves.

20'
20'

- Large, glossy, evergreen leaves
- Covered with white flower spikes in midspring
- Growth rate: slow to medium, 6 to 10 inches per year
- Zones 7 to 9, some cultivars to zone 6

This small tree is adaptable to both sun and shade, and can reach 20 feet tall and as wide. It is a favorite landscape plant on the West Coast. **USES:**. Use as a hedge or small flowering tree or plant along property lines as a screen.

SITING AND CARE: Plant in average soil and full sun to part shade. Roots are greedy; this is a difficult tree to garden under. Pruning is helpful to retain form, but it will delay blooming.

RELATED SPECIES: *P. caroliniana* (Carolina cherry laurel; zones 6 to 9), is a multistemmed tree with long, evergreen leaves. It reaches 40 feet tall and wide. *P. lusitanica* (Portuguese laurel; zone 7 to 9) is similar but with larger flower clusters.

Amur chokecherry (above left) and Prunus serrula (above right) both have impressive, lustrous bark.

PRUNUS MAACKII

PROO-nuss MACK-ee-eye

Amur chokecherry

20'
20'

- Unusual reddish brown bark with a metallic luster
- White flowers in spring
- Medium-size tree with rounded crown
- Growth rate: medium to fast, 15 to 18 inches per year
- Zones 3 to 6

Amur chokecherry has an interesting shape and habit, small flowers and fruit, and is very cold hardy. Native to Manchuria and Siberia. Will eventually reach up to 35 feet tall and as wide.

USES: Use as a specimen or accent tree, as a framing tree, or for shade for the patio or deck.

SITING AND CARE: Requires well-drained soil. This tree is more troublefree in the far North (zones 3 and 4) than farther south, and more valuable there as a substitute for the less-hardy paperbark maple (*Acer griseum*). *P. serrula* is a related species, also known for its shiny bark, with narrow leaves and single white flowers (zones 6 to 8).

of Sargent ...ast to the ...ly spring.

PRUNUS SARGENTII

PROO-nuss sar-JEN-tee-eye

Sargent cherry

25'
25'

- Clouds of pink flowers cover the tree in early spring
- Foliage turns bronzy red in fall
- Lustrous, reddish brown bark
- Growth rate: medium to fast, 15 to 18 inches per year
- Zones 5 to 8

An attractive harbinger of spring that grows well in northern climates, Sargent cherry is a tree with multiseason interest. Native to Japan and Korea. With age, it can reach 60 feet tall and wide.

USES: This is a nice-size tree for any part of the landscape—island planting, corner of the house, patio garden, or in a lawn as a specimen.

SITING AND CARE: Hardy tree that requires little maintenance or disease prevention. Prune to keep upright shape.

RECOMMENDED VARIETIES AND RELATED SPECIES: 'Columnaris' is narrow and upright. 'Accolade', a hybrid between *P. sargentii* and *P. subhirtella* (Higan cherry), is a vigorous upright tree 20 to 30 feet tall, with blush pink, semidouble flowers. Useful in zones 5 through 8.

PRUNUS HYBRIDS

PROO-nuss

Flowering cherry

12' / 12'

- Gorgeous, fragrant, white or pink flowers in spring
- Most cultivars are vase shaped and upright
- Growth rate: usually medium, but can be variable
- Zones 6 to 9, depending on the species and cultivar

Flowering cherries are the landmark tree for the Washington, D.C., area, and are among the most popular of flowering trees. Native to Japan, China, and Korea. Most reach 20 to 25 feet tall.

USES: Good for softening harsh corners; when massed in open areas, they attract birds and bring color and texture to the landscape as well.

SITING AND CARE: Plant in moist, well-drained soil. Inspect frequently for cankers.

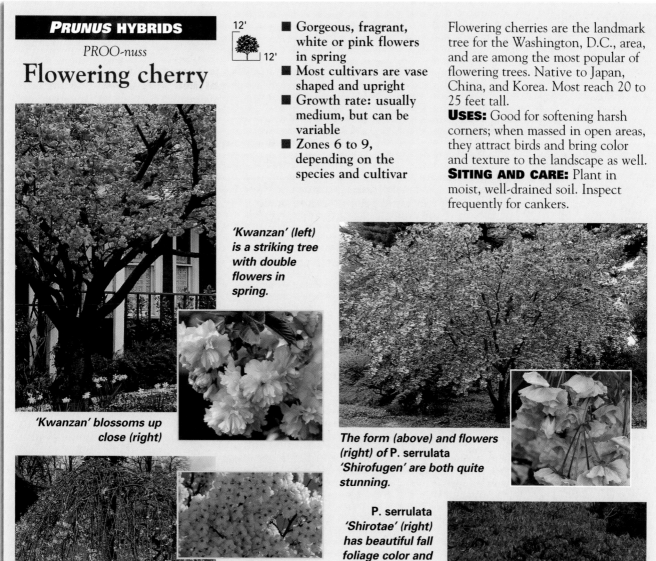

'Kwanzan' (left) is a striking tree with double flowers in spring.

'Kwanzan' blossoms up close (right)

The form (above) and flowers (right) of P. serrulata 'Shirofugen' are both quite stunning.

Yoshino cherry 'Akebone' (above) and 'Shidare yoshino' (left)

P. serrulata 'Shirotae' (right) has beautiful fall foliage color and wide-spreading, nearly pendulous form.

FLOWERING CHERRY CULTIVARS

Name	Flower Color	Tree Form	Size	Remarks
Japanese cherry (*P. serrulata*)	Pink	Vase-shaped	15 feet	Beautiful flowers and fall color
Sato-zakura hybrids				
'Amanogawa'	Pale pink	Upright	25 feet	Single to semi-double flowers
'Kwanzan'	Pink	Vase-shaped	30 feet	Large, very double flowers
'Shirotae'	White	Spreading	20 feet	Single to semi-double flowers
Higan cherry (*P. subhirtella*)	Pink	Spreading	15-25 feet	May have fall color some years
'Autumnalis'	White	Spreading	15 feet	May rebloom in fall in warm areas
'Pendula' (Weeping Higan)	Pale pink	Weeping	15 feet	Very popular for weeping form
'Whitcomb'	Pink	Globose	30 feet	Large cherry with single pink flowers
Yoshino cherry (*P. × yedoensis*)	White or pink	Open	40 feet	Washington, D.C.'s cherry
Okame cherry (*P. okame*)	Carmine-rose	Open	25 feet	Can color well in fall

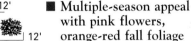

PSEUDOCYDONIA SINENSIS

soo-doh-sye-DOH-nee-ah sih-NEN-sis

Chinese quince

12'
12'

- Multiple-season appeal with pink flowers, orange-red fall foliage and winter bark
- Beautiful, gray-green-brown flaking bark
- Large (5- to 7-inch) bright yellow fruit
- Pink spring flowers
- Growth rate: slow, 8 to 10 inches per year
- Zones 6 to 9

With interesting flowers, fruit, structure, and bark, Chinese quince is a good performer in all seasons.

A useful small tree or large shrub, Chinese quince charms with its dainty flowers and earns attention year round with fall color, bright fruit, and attractive bark. Native to China. Grows 15 feet tall and wide.
USES: This is a great plant to use as a transition from the shrub border to the fruit garden with the added textural display of its peeling bark. If you're most interested in the bark, train it as a small tree.
SITING AND CARE: Best in moist, well-drained soil in full sun, with wind protection. Inspect frequently for fire blight. Prune out infected areas promptly or the fire blight may spread.

PSEUDOLARIX AMABILIS (KAEMPFERI)

soo-doh-LARE-icks ah-mah-BILL-iss

Golden larch

20'
10'

- Graceful, broadly pyramidal
- Deciduous conifer
- Feathery, light- to medium green foliage
- Growth rate: medium, 8 to 12 inches per year
- Zones 6 to 7, and milder areas of zone 5

When the needles of golden larch color in the fall, their mellow color draws a lot of attention.

This deciduous conifer is a graceful specimen with finely textured foliage that turns a golden yellow in the fall. Native to China. Can reach 60 feet tall and 30 feet wide.
USES: A good border or corner specimen for screening or background. It grows slowly enough to be positioned in most residential landscapes, and its broadly pyramidal shape is impressive. The fleshy cones add another season of interest in late summer.
SITING AND CARE: Best in cool-summer climates. Prefers moist, well-drained, slightly acidic soil in partial shade or full sun. Nearly a pestfree tree.

PSEUDOTSUGA MENZIESII

soo-dot-SOO-guh men-ZEE-see-eye

Douglas fir

18'
10'

- Upright evergreen conifer, with stately size and form
- Dark green to blue-green needles and small feathery cones
- Growth rate: medium, 8 to 12 inches per year
- Zones 4 to 6

Native to the Rocky Mountains and the Pacific coast, Douglas fir is used commercially as a Christmas tree. To 75 feet tall and 30 feet wide.

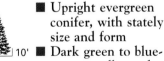

Often planted in groups, the Douglas fir has a strong enough structure to be used as a specimen also.

USES: Makes a good screen for patios, or use it as a single backyard specimen, upright accent, in mass plantings, or in groups.
SITING AND CARE: Needs full sun and well-drained, moist soil; struggles otherwise.
RECOMMENDED VARIETIES AND RELATED SPECIES: *P. menziesii.* subsp. *glauca* is the mountain form, slower growing and more cold hardy than the coastal form, and the one to use in the North and Midwest as well as colder areas of the West. It has bluish green foliage. 'Fastigiata' is a columnar selection of *glauca* and is useful for a vertical accent.

PYRUS CALLERYANA 'BRADFORD'

PYE-russ cah-lare-ee-AY-nuh

Callery pear

15'
10'

- White blossoms cover the tree before leaves emerge in midspring
- Lustrous, medium-green leaves turn red to purple in fall
- Growth rate: medium to fast
- Zones 5 to 8

A medium-size tree with many fine features, callery pear is native to Korea and China. Can reach 30 feet tall and 20 feet wide.

USES: Use in corner plantings, in parks, or as a street tree. Plant near small patios and backyard corners for immediate landscape impact.

SITING AND CARE: Best in full sun. Most cultivars of this species are highly resistant to fire blight.

RECOMMENDED VARIETIES:

'Aristocrat' is a large, narrowly pyramidal tree with strong crotch angles. Its fall foliage color is not quite as good as other cultivars, but it flowers nicely. 'Chanticleer' is smaller, upright, symmetrical tree. 'Redspire' is also pyramidal, with glossy, dark green leaves. In the North, its fall color is not as dependable. 'Bradford' was the first selection made of callery pear. Fo

The Bradford callery pear has showers of flowers early in the year, and blazing leaf color late.

PYRUS SALICIFOLIA

PYE-russ sah-liss-ih-FOH-lee-uh

Willow-leaved pear

10'
10'

- Pendulous small tree
- Graceful, willow-like, silver-grey leaves
- Growth rate: medium, 6 to 12 inches per year
- Zones 5 to 7

A fine landscape plant, native to southeastern Europe and western Asia. Can reach 15 feet tall.

USES: Used in a shrub border, its gray leaves blend well with most other colors. Accent a path where the leaves and branches can be in full view. Flowers are inconspicuous, and the few green fruits that do form add little interest.

SITING AND CARE: Susceptible to fire blight. Inspect and prune it out as it appears.

RECOMMENDED VARIETIES:
'Pendula' and Silver Frost® were selected for their strongly pendulous form.

The gray leaves and compact shape of willow-leaved pear combine well with brighter garden colors.

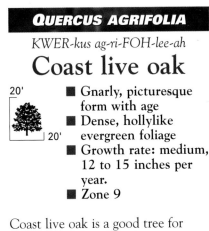

The lustrous, leathery leaves of coast live oak, which resemble holly, are a trademark of this tree.

QUERCUS AGRIFOLIA

KWER-kus ag-ri-FOH-lee-ah

Coast live oak

- Gnarly, picturesque form with age
- Dense, hollylike evergreen foliage
- Growth rate: medium, 12 to 15 inches per year.
- Zone 9

Coast live oak is a good tree for shade, much loved for its picturesque, gnarly form in old age. Native to the hills and mountains of coastal California. Can reach 50 feet tall and wide.

USES: A great shade tree, and a must for natural landscapes. This is not a good choice for lawns.

SITING AND CARE: Plant in well-drained soil and full sun to part shade; avoid overwatering in any season. Inspect tree for oak moth larvae. Acorns and leaf drop can be annoying. Oak root fungus can be devastating; always use mulch over root zone, never turf or flowers.

RELATED SPECIES: *Q. virginiana* (southern live oak; zones 8 to 9) is the signature tree of the Deep South for its spreading branches dripping with Spanish moss.

While it doesn't put on a pyrotechnic show in the fall, the leaves of white oak do color pleasantly.

QUERCUS ALBA

KWER-kuss AL-buh

White oak

- Large tree with outstanding durability and form
- Dark green leaves in summer, reddish purple in the fall
- Growth rate: slow to medium, 8 to 12 inches per year
- Zones 5 to 8, and milder parts of zone 4

A majestic tree with great shape and ruggedness, white oak is long lived and nearly pest free. Native to the East Coast, and west to the center of the United States. Can grow to 75 feet tall and wide.

USES: Good for shade and as a specimen if a large space is available. Needs the open spaces of estates, acreages, parks, and very large backyards.

SITING AND CARE: Grows best in well-drained soils.

RELATED SPECIES: *Q. bicolor* (swamp white oak) is almost as large and handsome as white oak, with greater tolerance of wet soils. It is hardy to zone 4.

Young shingle oaks often have a pyramidal form, but with age, they will broaden.

QUERCUS IMBRICARIA

KWER-kuss im-brih-KARE-ee-uh

Shingle oak

- Pyramidal when young; broad with age
- Medium to large tree, depending on site
- Lustrous dark green summer leaves turn tan in fall
- Growth rate: slow to medium, 8 to 12 inches per year
- Zones 5 to 8

A native oak, shingle oak is often underappreciated, but it is a nicely shaped, slow-growing tree. Native from the Ohio River valley to north Georgia and west to Iowa. With age, can reach 60 to 80 feet.

USES: Shingle oak makes an excellent shade tree for the larger lot. Grows well in the Midwest. It holds its dried foliage well into winter, and the leaves rustle in the wind. Similar in form to pin oak and a good substitute in soils that are not acidic. It can also be used as a hedge or screen.

SITING AND CARE: Prefers well-drained soils in full sun. Tolerant of dry soils.

QUERCUS MACROCARPA

KWER-kuss mack-roh-CAR-puh

Bur oak

20'

15'

- Large, stately tree
- Deeply ridged, furrowed, gnarled bark
- Young twigs covered with corky ridges
- Growth rate: slow to medium, 8 to 12 inches per year
- Zones 3 to 8

Bur oak is a fascinating tree, in a class by itself for rugged beauty. Native to eastern and central U. S.; grows to 90 feet with equal spread.

USES: Use it as a specimen shade tree. Requires open space and is good for a large acreage.
SITING AND CARE: This tree can be slow to develop, often needing 30 years to come into its mature form. Avoid turf over the root zone; use mulch instead.

Like a long-term investment, after many years burr oak pays off as a distinctive rugged tree.

QUERCUS PALUSTRIS

KWER-kuss pah-LUSS-triss

Pin oak

25'

15'

- Sturdy, storm-resistant branches on a pyramidal tree
- Lustrous, dark green foliage changes to reddish brown in fall
- Growth rate: medium to fast; 10 to 15 inches per year
- Zones 5 to 8, and milder areas of zone 4

One of the fastest-growing oaks, pin oak is native from New England west to Wisconsin and south to Arkansas. Up to 75 feet tall.
USES: Popular due to relatively fast growth rate, fall color, and sturdy branches, pin oak is a good backyard shade tree.
SITING AND CARE: Grows best in acidic soils. Susceptible to iron chlorosis in limestone soils.
RELATED SPECIES: *Q. coccinea,* (scarlet oak) is similar to pin oak, but more rounded and open at maturity, with more reliable red fall color. It is more tolerant of soils with high pH.

Pin oak is one of the fastest-growing oaks.

QUERCUS PHELLOS

KWER-kuss FEH-lohss

Willow oak

20'

15'

- Light, bright green, willow-shaped leaves
- Pyramidal when maturing; rounded with age
- Fine-textured foliage turns yellow in fall
- Growth rate: medium, 10 to 15 inches per year
- Zones 6 to 9

Native from the eastern seaboard west to Missouri and Texas, willow oak is one of the best oaks for the South. With age, it grows up to 50 feet tall and 40 feet wide.
USES: A magnificent street tree, entryway marker, or backyard shade tree, and is useful in other large spaces. Similar in shape to pin oak.
SITING AND CARE: Best in moist, well-drained soil but adapts to most soil sites.

The leaves of willow oak give it its name.

Willow oak commands attention as a street tree, its strong trunk and limbs dominating the landscape.

Mature specimens of English oak have impressive trunks and an appealing bold texture.

QUERCUS ROBUR

KWER-kuss ROH-burr

English oak

- Best known in the U.S. for good columnar forms
- Coarse texture
- Deeply furrowed and fissured bark
- Growth rate: slow, 6 to 8 inches per year
- Zones 6 to 8, and milder areas of zone 5

A grand and stately tree, English oak is native to Europe. With age, it can reach 60 feet tall and as wide.

USES: Good for the small-to-medium-size landscape, this oak will mature so slowly that landscape renovation will likely be called for by the time it is too large.

For most of the U. S. and Canada, native oaks are faster growing and perform better, but the narrow cultivars of English oak are of interest (see below).

SITING AND CARE: Requires full sun and moist, well-drained soil.

RECOMMENDED VARIETIES: 'Fastigiata' is a fine columnar tree for a strong vertical accent. Skymaster™ and Skyrocket™ have similar columnar shapes.

The best oak for the conditions of the Midwest, red oak leaves can color subtly or brightly in fall.

QUERCUS RUBRA

KWER-kuss ROO-brah

Northern red oak

- Lustrous, dark leaves turn red in fall
- Upright and rounded when young, rounded and symmetrical when older
- Foliage canopy is moderately open in youth, denser with age
- Growth rate: medium to fast, 12 to 15 inches per year
- Zones 4 to 8

One of the best oaks for growing in the Midwest, red oak is native from Maine and Minnesota to Georgia. Mature trees can reach 75 feet tall and as wide.

USES: This fast-growing, large specimen makes an excellent shade tree for the backyard, patio, or deck area, or for use as a specimen.

SITING AND CARE: Best in full sun and moist but well-drained soil. Relatively pest free.

RELATED SPECIES: *Q. shumardii* (Shumard oak), native from the Midwest and East to the Carolinas, differs only in bud form, color, and size. It is strongly pyramidal but spreads with age. In most locations, it will grow to 50 to 55 feet tall. Fall color can be a nice russet red to bright red depending on the conditions.

ROBINIA PSEUDOACACIA

roh-BIN-ee-ah soo-doh-uh-KAY-see-ah

Black locust

25'
10'

- Clusters of fragrant white flowers in spring
- Rough and fissured bark; can be covered with large thorns
- Growth rate: medium to fast, 10 to 15 inches per year
- Zones 3 to 8

Black locust is a good for poor soils and other difficult conditions. Native from the Ohio River valley west to Iowa and naturalized elsewhere. Mature specimens can be 75 feet tall and 30 feet wide.

USES: Reclaimed sites, parks, landfills, strip mines, cemeteries, etc. Cultivars should be considered.

SITING AND CARE: Adapts to dry and unfertile soils. While it can sucker profusely, no special care is needed to maintain health.

RECOMMENDED VARIETIES AND RELATED SPECIES: 'Frisia' has golden yellow leaves in summer. 'Umbraculifera' (globe or umbrella black locust) is a small tree to 15 feet tall. *R. × ambigua* includes hybrids of *R. pseudoacacia* such as 'Idahoensis' and 'Purple Robe', which are rose-pink flowering trees to 30 to 40 feet tall.

R. pseudoacacia 'Frisia'

SALIX ALBA VAR. TRISTIS

SAY-licks AL-buh

Golden weeping willow

25'
25'

- Large, rounded, weeping form
- Yellow-gold branches
- Growth rate: fast to extremely fast, 18 to 24 inches per year
- Zones 3 to 8

A tree for wet sites, golden willow is native to Europe and some parts of Africa and Asia. Can grow to 75 feet tall and as wide.

USES: Not really for the home landscape, except on large acreages.

SITING AND CARE: Most vigorous in moist soil. Requires constant cleanup of fallen limbs; roots invade and damage drainage and septic lines.

RELATED SPECIES: *S. pentandra* (laurel willow) is a medium-size, oval tree with shiny branches and stems, and lustrous, dark green foliage. In the humid South, foliar disease can completely defoliate the tree by midsummer, which limits its use. *S. babylonica* (Babylon weeping willow; milder areas of zone 6 to 8) is a medium-size, 35- to 50-foot tree with similar characteristics and form.

In wet areas with lots of room, nothing is quite as impressive as a golden weeping willow.

SALIX MATSUDANA 'TORTUOSA'

SAY-licks matt-soo-DAH-nuh

Corkscrew willow

15'
10'

- Curiously twisted and contorted branches and stems
- Grows 25 feet tall
- Narrow, bright green leaves, 3 to 4 inches long
- Growth rate: fast, 18 to 24 inches per year
- Zones 4 to 8

Corkscrew willow is a good conversation piece, with an interesting winter appearance. Its foliage and stems are used in flower arrangements. The species is native to northern China. Can rapidly reach up to 25 feet tall and wide.

USES: Place this medium-sized tree near a patio or along a path with its contorted branches and stems in full view (but not near a pool, due to extensive limb and stem droppage).

SITING AND CARE: Tolerates a wide range of soils. Experiences dieback in winters with fluctuating temperatures, as in Nebraska, Iowa, Kansas, and Illinois.

With its wildly twisted branches, corkscrew willow is a powerful winter-interest tree.

A small tree with many uses in the landscape, Chinese tallow tree often colors nicely in the fall.

SAPIUM SEBIFERUM

SAY-pee-um seh-BIH-fer-um

Chinese tallow tree

25' / 15'

- Dense, thick foliage, yet produces a slightly open, airy appearance
- Dark green leaves coupled with yellow, stringlike flowers
- Good fall color
- Medium-sized, rounded tree
- Growth rate: fast, 12 to 18 inches per year
- Zones 8 to 10

Chinese tallow tree is rapid growing and a good replacement for poplars, as it encounters fewer pests. Fall color can be quite strong in some years. Native to China, Japan, and Korea. Can grow to 40 feet tall.
USES: A fast-growing, medium-sized tree for quick shade. Over decks and patios or in terrace gardens flower and fruit litter can be a problem. Useful as screening on property lines due to its rapid growth.
SITING AND CARE: Prune when young to produce a single trunk with a strong central leader; or allow it to grow in its natural form. Relatively pest free. Can become weedy in the Deep South.

SASSAFRAS ALBIDUM

SASS-uh-frass al-BYE-dum

Sassafras

25' / 20'

- Bright green leaves in summer change to neon colors in fall
- Haze of yellow flowers is effective in early spring before leaves
- Growth rate: medium to fast, 12 to 18 inches per year
- Zones 5 to 9

Over time, a grove of sassafras in full fall glory can rival almost any native tree for impact.

Common to hedgerows and woodlands of the eastern U. S., sassafras is a native tree best known for its blazing fall color. Will grow as a multitrunked thicket if not pruned back. Native from Canada to Florida and west to Texas. Grows to 60 feet tall.
USES: Use it along paths, in thickets, mass plantings, and corner landscape plantings, where the fall colors and early spring flowers can be seen up close.
SITING AND CARE: Can be difficult to transplant; acquire container-grown plants. Prefers moist, well-drained, slightly acidic soils. Remove suckers if single tree form is desired.

SCHINUS MOLLE

SKY-nuss moll

Pepper tree

20' / 20'

- Picturesque form and shape, gracefully drooping branches
- Bright evergreen, fine-textured leaves
- Attractive red berries
- Can be messy with dropping leaves, fruits, and stems
- Growth rate: fast
- Zones 9 to 10

The combination of exotic, dark green leaves and bright fruit calls much attention to the pepper tree.

A fast-growing ornamental shade tree native to Peru, Bolivia, and Chile. Can grow up to 50 feet tall.
USES: Great for fast shade and asymmetrical form. Can also be planted closely and sheared for a hedge. Fine tree for informal patios, to shade play areas, or in areas with poor soil. Unfortunately, drawbacks include weak wood that drops branches and much litter, and greedy roots that will seek out septic and sewer lines.
SITING AND CARE: Has surface rooting habit and will drop litter, making it a poor choice next to sidewalks and driveways. Susceptible to scale and aphids.

SCIADOPITYS VERTICILLATA

sky-uh-DAW-pi-tis ver-tih-sih-LAY-tuh

Japanese umbrella pine

10'
4'

- Small refined conifer
- Whorled needles create an umbrella-shaped terminal
- Growth rate: very slow, 3 to 5 inches per year
- Zones 4 to 8

An outstanding specimen, this native of Japan has been growing in popularity for its slow, restrained growth and easy-care nature. It can be grown as bonsai. Can reach 25 to 40 feet after many years.

USES: Its slow growth makes it easy to incorporate into rock gardens, shrub borders, and near patios. Be sure to site it with close-up viewing in mind.

SITING AND CARE: Locate it in moist, rich soil in areas where morning and midday sun give way to late afternoon shade. Provide some wind protection.

The whorled leaves of Japanese umbrella pine are interesting when viewed up close.

SEQUOIA SEMPERVIRENS

seh-KWOY-yuh sem-per-VYE-renz

Coast redwood

20'
15'

- Narrow, pyramidal form
- Small attractive needles grow in spirals
- Extremely large on the West Coast
- Fresh looking and woodsy smelling
- Growth rate: fast initially, slower with age
- Zones 7 to 9

Useful only on the Pacific coast, where it is native to northern California. Mature trees can be over 100 feet tall.

USES: Plant it where it has room to grow—on the perimeter of a large lawn or other expansive area.

SITING AND CARE: Grows well in cool locations and in moist, acidic soils. Needs frequent watering; does not tolerate drought.

RELATED SPECIES: *Sequoiadendron giganteum* (giant sequoia; zones 7 to 9) is useful both in the West and in the Middle Atlantic area as well as California, where it is native. It reaches 75 feet in the East, with a handsome, buttressed trunk and red bark.

In California, coast redwood grows quickly when young. Mature stands are known to be 2,000 years old.

SOPHORA JAPONICA

soh-FOR-ruh ja-PON-ih-kuh

Japanese pagoda tree

20'
20'

- Creamy white summer flowers
- Good filtered shade
- Medium-sized tree requiring little care
- Growth rate: medium to fast, 12 to 15 inches per year
- Zones 6 to 8, and milder areas of zone 5

This wonderful summer-blooming tree with large white flowers is native to China and Korea. Can grow to 75 feet tall and wide.

USES: Good choice over patios for shade and late-summer flowers.

SITING AND CARE: Best in sun and average, well-drained soil. Tolerates urban sites with poor soils.

RECOMMENDED VARIETIES AND RELATED SPECIES: 'Pendula', a weeping form with bright green branches in winter, is a good accent tree. 'Regent' has a fast growth rate and a large, rounded, oval crown. *S. secundiflora* (mescal bean; zones 8 to 9) is a small, 25-foot tree with long clusters of violet-blue flowers in early spring.

Japanese pagoda tree 'Regent' offers light, filtered shade under a broad crown.

Delicate dark green foliage sets the perfect backdrop for the bright fruits of European mountain ash.

SORBUS AUCUPARIA

SORE-buss awk-yoo-PARE-ee-uh

European mountain ash

20' / 15'

- Bright orange fruit in summer and fall
- White spring flowers
- Fine foliage texture
- Good reddish fall foliage color
- Growth rate: medium, 10 to 12 inches per year
- Zones 3 to 6

Small, with an upright habit, European mountain ash is native to Europe and western Asia. Best in zones 3 and 4. Can grow to 30 feet. **USES:** Accent the patio garden or courtyard with this tree. **SITING AND CARE:** Plant in cool, moist, well-drained soils. Cankers and borers are serious problems, especially in zones 5 and 6. Wrap young trunks to protect from scald. **RECOMMENDED VARIETIES AND RELATED SPECIES:** 'Cardinal Royal' is a vigorous grower with an upright, narrow-oval habit. Korean mountain ash (*Sorbus alnifolia*) is larger, to 50 feet tall, free of borers, but susceptible to fire blight in some areas. Has red-orange fall foliage and silvery gray bark in addition to bright fruit.

Known mainly for its camellia-like summer flowers, Japanese stewartia also has fall color and showy bark.

STEWARTIA PSEUDOCAMELLIA

stew-AHR-tee-uh soo-doh-kah-MEE-lee-uh

Japanese stewartia

15' / 12'

- White midsummer flowers like camellias
- Dark green leaves turn bronze to purple in fall
- Outstanding multicolored bark
- Growth rate: Slow, 8 to 12 inches per year
- Zones 6 to 7

A magnificent ornamental tree, offering interest in every season of the year. Native to Japan. Can reach 40 feet tall and as wide. **USES:** This small- to medium-size beauty has a number of uses—in the patio, landscape border, and shrub border. It can be wonderful in a mixed flower garden for a strong vertical effect. **SITING AND CARE:** Grows best in acidic soils that are well drained. Check pH and correct if needed. **RECOMMENDED VARIETIES AND RELATED SPECIES:** 'Korean Splendor' (also called *S. koreana*) is exceptional in its flowers and bark interest and is cold hardy in the mildest areas of zone 5.

Delicate, bell-shaped flowers, either in pink or white, attract attention to Japanese snowbell in early summer.

STYRAX JAPONICUS

STY-racks ja-PON-ih-kuss

Japanese snowbell

15' / 15'

- Lovely rounded low-branched tree
- White, pendulous flowers bloom in early summer
- Small, clean and tidy, with dense foliage
- Growth rate: slow
- Zones 7 to 8, and milder areas of zone 6

This little-known tree from Japan deserves considerable landscape use. With age, to 20 to 25 feet tall.

USES: Its branches hanging over a patio can be quite impressive. Use it in small gardens, near decks or other outdoor entertaining areas, and in courtyards where you can look up into the flowers. **SITING AND CARE:** Needs frequent watering and pruning to retain desired shape. **RECOMMENDED VARIETIES AND RELATED SPECIES:** 'Pendula' ('Carillon') is semi-weeping and has impressive flowers and foliage. 'Pink Chimes' has pink flowers and is semipendulous. Fragrant snowbell (*S. obassia*; zones 6 to 8) is more upright, to 35 feet tall, with larger, rounded leaves and larger clusters of fragrant flowers.

SYRINGA RETICULATA

sih-RING-guh reh-tick-yoo-LAY-tuh

Japanese tree lilac

15'
15'

- Dense, upright to pyramidal, small tree
- Covered with white plume-shaped flowers in early summer
- Dark green, thick, oval to slightly heart-shaped leaves
- Growth rate: medium, 8 to 10 inches per year
- Zones 3 to 7

This is a care-free, reliable, tough performer for the Midwest, the East, and for some western climates. Native to Japan and parts of China. Grows to 30 feet tall.

USES: Excellent for the shrub border, in masses for screening, or as an accent; also good as a small street tree and for the entryway or corner of a home. Tends to flower well only every other year.

SITING AND CARE: In full sun for best flowering. Relatively pestfree.

RECOMMENDED VARIETIES: 'Ivory Silk' flowers at a young age and is sturdy and compact. 'Summer Snow' is compact, with a rounded crown and abundant flowers.

Abundant white flowers show off against the dark green leaves of Japanese tree lilac in summer.

TAMARIX RAMOSISSIMA

TAM-uh-ricks ram-oh-SISS-ih-muh

Five-stamen tamarisk

12'
12'

- Loose, multistemmed, shrublike appearance
- Small, rosy pink flowers that cover the long branches
- Very fine, juniperlike foliage
- Growth rate: fast growing, 12 to 18 inches per year
- Zones 4 to 8, and in milder areas of zone 3

A small tree adaptable to many sites, five-stamen tamarisk tolerates both cold and heat. Native to southeastern Europe and central Asia. Can grow to 16 feet tall.

USES: This tree makes a good shrub border plant, but because of its open form, it is better used in masses than as a single specimen.

SITING AND CARE: Prefers well-drained, low-fertility soils in full sun. Will bloom in partial shade but not nearly as abundantly. Tolerant of many soil types, including saline soils.

RECOMMENDED VARIETIES: 'Cheyenne Red' and 'Summer Glow' have deep-pink flowers.

The rosy pink flowers of five-stamen tamarisk profusely decorate the open form of this small tree.

TAXODIUM DISTICHUM

tack-SOH-dee-um DISS-tih-kum

Bald cypress

30'
15'

- A deciduous conifer
- Foliage turns russet-red in late fall
- Attractive reddish brown bark on a buttressed trunk
- Growth rate: medium to fast, 18 to 24 inches per year
- Zones 3 to 10

Native to the southeastern U.S. It can reach 100 feet tall and 40 feet wide.

USES: Requires room to grow. Excellent specimen tree.

SITING AND CARE: Grow in full sun. May be a bit iron-chlorotic under high pH conditions.

Bald cypress is a good tree for wet sites and has many other fine features for use in the landscape.

Bald cypress is easily recognized by its knobby "knees" wide, flaring trunk, and fall color.

THUJA OCCIDENTALIS

THOO-ya ock-sih-den-TAL-is

American arborvitae

With its conical shape and bright green foliage, American arborvitae is a garden favorite everywhere.

12' / 3'
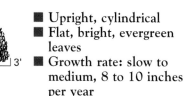

- Upright, cylindrical
- Flat, bright, evergreen leaves
- Growth rate: slow to medium, 8 to 10 inches per year
- Zones 4 to 8

A good evergreen for adding upright form in the landscape, its dense foliage makes an effective screen. Native to northeastern North America from Nova Scotia south to North Carolina. Can reach 40 feet tall and 15 feet wide.

USES: Makes a good screen but not a good windbreak—it will burn with excessive cold winter wind and sun. It is good for the larger shrub or garden border and will tolerate wet or poorly-drained sites.

SITING AND CARE: Grows best in partial sun with wind protection. Can be sheared if desired.

RECOMMENDED VARIETIES AND RELATED SPECIES: 'Techny' is pyramidal with very dark leaves. 'Emerald' ('Smaragd') has bright-green foliage and symmetrical, pyramidal form. *Thuja plicata* (giant or western arborvitae) has slender, drooping branches. Reaches 200 feet in Pacific coastal areas, usually 80 feet in gardens. Inland forms perform well in the Midwest as windbreaks and are not eaten by deer, unlike *T. occidentalis*.

TILIA CORDATA

TILL-ee-uh kor-DAY-tuh

Littleleaf linden

The oddly shaped pale flowers of littleleaf linden stand out against the darker foliage.

20' / 10'
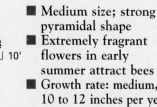

- Medium size; strong pyramidal shape
- Extremely fragrant flowers in early summer attract bees
- Growth rate: medium, 10 to 12 inches per year
- Zones 4 to 7, and milder areas of zone 3

In addition to its pleasing, pyramidal shape and fine foliage, littleleaf linden casts dense shade and grows well in most conditions. Native to Europe. Mature trees can reach a height of 75 feet with a spread of 40.

USES: A good framing tree for the backyard or shade from the street side (and in other areas) if enough root space is provided.

SITING AND CARE: Needs well-drained, loose soil. Tolerates periods of dry weather; plant in low-maintenance landscapes. Will develop girdling roots in compacted sites, and it is severely damaged by Japanese beetles.

RECOMMENDED VARIETIES AND RELATED SPECIES: Shamrock™ has a more open crown than the species but retains its strong pyramidal shape. 'Greenspire' is a popular cultivar with dark green foliage; it is a hardy tree that grows well in difficult conditions. It is, however, extremely susceptible to Japanese beetles in the Midwest.

TILIA TOMENTOSA

TILL-ee-uh toh-men-TOH-suh

Silver linden

Silver linden's leaves, dark on top and light on the underside, create an interesting effect even in light wind.

25' / 15'

- Classic pyramidal linden shape
- Silver undersides of dark-green leaves
- Very fragrant, small flowers
- Growth rate: medium, 10 to 14 inches per year
- Zones 5 to 7

Silver linden adds a silvery sheen to the landscape in summer. Native to southeastern Europe and western Asia. Can grow 75 feet tall.

USES: A good shade or framing tree for larger landscapes, especially where the silver leaves are easily seen. Its tolerance of dry conditions also makes it a good street tree.

SITING AND CARE: No special care is required. May develop girdling roots in compacted soils.

RECOMMENDED VARIETIES AND RELATED SPECIES: 'Wandell' ('Sterling Silver®') has lustrous, dark green leaves and is resistant to Japanese beetle and gypsy moth. 'Green Mountain®' is a rapid grower, with a dense canopy, and is heat and drought tolerant. *Tilia × flavescens* 'Redmond' (Redmond linden) exhibits dense medium green foliage on a rounded, broad canopy. It grows about 8 to 10 inches per year, eventually to 40 to 50 feet.

TSUGA CANADENSIS

SOO-guh can-uh-DEN-siss

Canadian hemlock

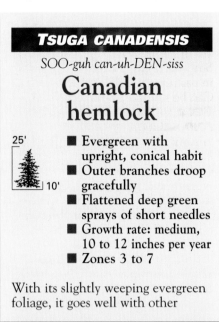

25'

10'

- Evergreen with upright, conical habit
- Outer branches droop gracefully
- Flattened deep green sprays of short needles
- Growth rate: medium, 10 to 12 inches per year
- Zones 3 to 7

With its slightly weeping evergreen foliage, it goes well with other plants grouped in semi-shade. Native from southern Canada south to Georgia along mountain ranges. Can grow to 90 feet tall.

USES: Grows well in groupings in odd-numbered masses, and makes a fine formal hedge, background planting, or screen. Goes well in semishaded gardens with astilbe, fothergilla, clethra, or coral bells planted nearby.

SITING AND CARE: Needs cool, moist conditions in full sun with protection, or in medium shade. Some native stands of Canadian hemlock in the Northeast have been badly damaged by wooly adelgid insects. Inspect for them in landscape plantings.

RECOMMENDED VARIETIES AND RELATED SPECIES: *T. caroliniana* (Carolina hemlock), zones 6 to 7, is also susceptible to woolly adelgids.

Besides its graceful habit and attractive foliage, Canadian hemlock is also known for tolerating shade.

ULMUS AMERICANA

UHL-muss uh-mare-ih-KAY-nuh

American elm

30'

20'

- Vase-shaped winter silhouette
- Thick, dense foliage produces heavy shade
- Growth rate: fast, 14 to 20 inches per year
- Zones 3 to 9, and milder areas of zone 2

A classic American tree, American elm is a stately tree for large areas. Native from the eastern seaboard west to the Rocky Mountains.

Mature specimens can grow up to 100 feet tall or more.

USES: Useful on large estates where it can grow without too much competition.

SITING AND CARE: Susceptible to elm leaf miners, elm leaf beetles, stem cankers, bacterial wet wood, and especially to Dutch elm disease (DED) and elm yellows (phloem necrosis). Best to keep trees healthy through judicious pruning and debris removal.

RECOMMENDED VARIETIES AND RELATED SPECIES: It remains to be seen how resistant new cultivars will be to Dutch elm disease and elm yellows. Large-scale planting is not advised.

Healthy, mature American elms can create an unforgettable vista in a large-scale planting.

ULMUS PARVIFOLIA

UHL-muss pahr-vih-FOH-lee-uh

Chinese elm or lacebark elm

20'

12'

- American-elm shape without susceptibility to most elm diseases
- Magnificent bark; mottled gray, green, orange, and brown
- Good bronze fall color
- Growth rate: medium to fast, 8 to 12 inches per year
- Zones 6 to 9, and milder areas of zone 5

Native to China, Korea, and Japan, Chinese elm is a good medium-sized tree for patio shade. It can reach 50 feet tall and 30 feet wide.

USES: Plant Chinese elm where one can view the bark easily.

SITING AND CARE: Best in moist, well-drained soils but tolerant of poor, dry soils. Shows considerable resistance to Dutch elm disease and to elm leaf beetle.

RECOMMENDED VARIETIES: Several cultivars were introduced in the 1990s and are under evaluation for cold hardiness in different regions. Consult your local nursery or extension office.

Much like its American cousin, Chinese elm is a striking tree, but it has better disease resistance and attractive bark.

Spiky lavender blooms arch above the rounded shape of chaste trees in summer bloom.

VITEX AGNUS-CASTUS

VYE-tex ag-nuss-KASS-tuss

Chaste tree

20'
20'

- Broad and spreading; usually multitrunked
- Prominent 6-inch, lavender flower spikes appear in summer
- Growth rate: slow in the north, fast in warmer areas, 1 to 3 feet per year
- Zones 7 to 9

Native to southern Europe and western Asia, chaste tree is good for patio shade when trained as a tree instead of a bush. Flowers and foliage exude spicy fragrance. Can reach 25 to 30 feet tall.

USES: Good for the patio and for summer color in the shrub border.

SITING AND CARE: Best flowering in full sun and hot conditions; pale flowers result from cool shade. Tolerates arid soils, but growth is best with adequate water. Prune to a single stem for patio shade or for the shrub border. Will die back to the ground periodically north of zone 7 but will return to flower as a shrub, and is useful in this way to zone 5.

RECOMMENDED VARIETIES: Cultivars with blue, pink, and white flowers are seldom available.

ZELKOVA SERRATA

zel-KOH-vuh sare-AH-tuh

Japanese zelkova

Reminiscent of elms, Japanese zelkovas have deep green leaves that color well in the fall.

20'
15'

- Vase-shape form similar to American elm
- Deep summer greens turn shades of red and yellow in fall
- Somewhat resistant to Dutch elm disease
- Growth rate: medium, 8 to 12 inches per year
- Zones 6 to 8, and milder areas of zone 5

Native to Japan and Korea, this tree should be considered if elm shape is desired, as it has better disease resistance than the elms. May reach 75 feet tall and 50 feet wide.

USES: Good tree for framing and for shade in the urban landscape.

SITING AND CARE: Select specimens with good branching structure in the nursery, as this can be variable in zelkova. Prune to retain desirable shape. A good medium-sized shade tree.

RECOMMENDED VARIETIES AND RELATED SPECIES: 'Green Vase' is vase-shaped with upright, arching branches. It is a vigorous tree with orange to bronze-red fall color. 'Halka' is fast growing with a graceful vase-shaped form similar to American elm. 'Village Green' is a pest-resistant tree with rusty red fall color. The relatively new 'Illinois Hardy' may prove more cold hardy than average, based on early experience.

ZIZIPHUS JUJUBA

ZIH-zih-fuss joo-JOO-buh

Chinese date or Chinese jujuba

The colorful fruits of Chinese date hang heavily on the pendulous branches.

15'
5'

- Irregularly vase-shaped tree, to 25 feet tall
- Spiny, gnarled, pendulous branches
- Clusters of small yellow flowers appear in early summer
- Growth rate: slow to medium, 6 to 10 inches per year
- Zones 6 to 9

Its interesting shape, foliage, fruit, flowers, and hardiness make it a good choice for many mild-climate landscapes. Native to southeastern Europe and China. Can eventually grow 30 feet tall.

USES: Chinese date tree is a good accent tree for the small landscape.

SITING AND CARE: Best in moist, fertile soils. Will tolerate dry, salty soils. Prune in winter to encourage weeping habit.

INDEX

Page numbers in italics denote photographs. Boldface numbers refer to lead entries in the "Selection and Growing Guide."

A

Abies concolor, **45**. See White fir
Acer ginnala (Amur maple), **46**
Acer griseum, **46**. See Paperbark maple
Acer negundo, **46**. See Box elder
Acer palmatum, **47**. See Japanese maple
Acer platanoides, **47**. See Norway maple
Acer rubrum, **48**. See Red maple
Acer saccharinum, **48**. See Silver maple
Acer saccharum, **48**. See Sugar maple
Aesculus glabra (Ohio buckeye), **49**
Aesculus hippocastanum, **49**. See Horsechestnut, common
Aesculus × carnea, **49**. See Red horsechestnut
Air pollution, 6, 28, 29
Albizia julibrissin, **50**. See Silk tree
Alder (*Alnus*), 6, 32
   European black, **50**
Allée, 8, *13*
Allegheny serviceberry (*Amelanchier laevis*), 16–17, **50**

Alnus glutinosa (European black alder), **50**
Amelanchier × grandiflora, **50**. See Apple serviceberry
Amendments, soil, 36
American arborvitae (*Thuja occidentalis*), 13, 24–25, **90**
American beech (*Fagus grandifolia*), 15, 23, **62**
American elm (*Ulmus americana*), **91**
American holly (*Ilex opaca*), **65**
American hornbeam (*Carpinus caroliniana*), **52**
Amur chokecherry (*Prunus maackii*), **78**
Amur cork tree (*Phellodendron amurense*), **72**
Amur maple (*Acer ginnala*), **46**
Anthracnose, 56
Aphids, 45, 57, 77, 86
Apple serviceberry (*Amelanchier × grandiflora*), 16–17, **50**
Appraisers, tree, 5
Arborists, 43
Arborvitae. See American arborvitae
Argyle apple (*Eucalyptus cinerea*), 60, **61**
Arizona cypress (*Cupressus arizonica*), **58**
Ash (*Fraxinus*), **63**
Asimina triloba (Pawpaw), **51**
Atlas cedar (*Cedrus libani atlantica*), **53**
Austrian pine (*Pinus nigra*), 6, **74**

B

Bald cypress (*Taxodium distichum*), 15, **89**
Balled-and-burlapped trees, 35, 36
Balsam fir (*Abies balsamea*), **45**
Bare-root trees, 35, 36, 38
Bark appearance, 23
Beech (*Fagus*), **62**. See American beech; European beech
Betula nigra, **51**. See River birch
Betula pendula (European white birch), **51**
Bigleaf magnolia (*Magnolia macrophylla*), 18, 29, **68**
Birch (*Betula*), 8, 13, 14, 23, **51**. See Paper birch; River birch
Black gum (*Nyssa sylvatica*), 22, **71**
Black locust (*Robinia pseudoacacia*), 19, 20, **85**
Black walnut (*Juglans nigra*), **65**
Blue gum (*Eucalyptus globulus*), 61
Blue noble fir (*Abies procera* 'Glauca'), **45**
Blue spruce. See Colorado blue spruce
Borers, 77
Bottlebrush (*Callistemon*), 18, **52**
Boundaries, defining, 8, 9
Box elder (*Acer negundo*), 20, **46**
Bristlecone pine, 15
Broadleaf evergreen trees, 24–25
Buckeye, Ohio (*Aesculus glabra*), **49**
Bur oak (*Quercus macrocarpa*), **83**
Buying trees, 34–35

MAIL ORDER SOURCES

Shopping for trees from catalogs is becoming more popular as the list of reputable mail-order nurseries grows. Catalogs offer a diverse selection and some offer hard-to-find varieties. Many are full of helpful information and advice. Finally, you can order ahead of the season from mail-order nurseries so your tree will be shipped to you at the proper time.

Appalachian Gardens
P.O. Box 87
410 Westview Avenue
Waynesboro, PA 17268-0087
717-762-4312, 888-327-5483
Hardy ornamental trees, many dogwoods

Carroll Gardens
444 E. Main St.
Westminster, MD 21157
800-638-6334
Conifers and ornamental trees

Eastern Plant Specialties
P.O. Box 226
Georgetown, ME 04548
207-371-2888

General, ornamental trees

Forestfarm
990 Tetherow Road
Williams, OR 97544-9599
541-846-7269
Collectors' selection of trees, many western natives

Gossler Farms Nursery
1200 Weaver Road
Springfield, OR 97478-3922
541-746-6611
General

Greer Gardens
1280 Goodpasture Island Road
Eugene, OR 97401-1794
541-686-8266
Wide selection of unusual trees, many Japanese maples, magnolias, stewartias, franklinias, beeches

Heronswood Nursery
7530 NE 288th Street
Kingston, WA 98346-9502
360-297-4172
Wide selection, many maples, cercidiphyllum, willows, conifers

Roslyn Nursery
211 Burrs Lane
Dix Hills, NY 11746
516-643-9347
Ornamental trees

Wayside Gardens
P.O. Box 1
Hodges, SC 29695-0001
800-845-1124
General, ornamental trees

Woodlanders
1128 Colleton Ave.
Aiken, SC 29801
803-648-7522
Rare and hard-to-find trees, many southeastern natives

Yucca Do Nursery
P.O. Box 5104
Hempstead, TX 77445
409-826-4580
Shrubs and plants for the Southwest

C

Callery pear (*Pyrus calleryana*), 13, 16–17, 18, **81**

Callistemon citrinus, **52**. See Lemon bottlebrush

Camphor tree (*Cinnamomum camphora*), **55**

Canadian hemlock (*Tsuga canadensis*), **91**

Cankers, 77

Carolina cherry laurel (*Prunus caroliniana*), **78**

Carolina silverbell (*Halesia tetraptera*), 18, **64**

Carpinus betulus, **52**. See European hornbeam

Carya illinoinensis (Pecan), **52**

Catalpa bignonioides, **53**. See Southern catalpa

Cedar of Lebanon (*Cedrus libani*), **53**

Cedrus libani atlantica (Atlas cedar), **53**

Celtis occidentalis (Common hackberry), **53**

Cercidiphyllum japonicum (Katsura tree), *42*, **54**

Cercis canadensis, **54**. See Eastern redbud

Chamaecyparis lawsoniana (Lawson false cypress), **54**

Chaste tree (*Vitex agnus-castus*), 19, **92**

Cherry, flowering (*Prunus hybrids*), **79**

Cherry, Higan (*Prunus subhirtella*), 18, **78–79**

Cherry, Japanese flowering (*Prunus serrulata*), 16–17, 18

Cherry laurel (*Prunus laurocerasus*), **78**

Cherry plum (*Prunus cerasifera*), 18, **77**

Chinese date (*Ziziphus jujuba*), **92**

Chinese elm (*Ulmus parvifolia*), 23, **91**

Chinese jujuba. See Chinese date

Chinese pistachio (*Pistacia chinensis*), **76**

Chinese quince (*Pseudocydonia sinensis*), 16–17, **80**

Chinese tallow tree (*Sapium sebiferum*), **86**

Chionanthus virginicus, **55**. See White fringe tree

Cider gum (*Eucalyptus gunnii*), **61**

Cinnamomum camphora (Camphor tree), **55**

Cladrastis lutea, **55**. See Yellowwood

Climate, 26–27, 30

Coast live oak (*Quercus agrifolia*), **82**

Coast redwood (*Sequoia sempervirens*), 15, **87**

Cockspur hawthorn (*Crataegus crus-galli*), **57**

Colorado blue spruce (*Picea pungens glauca*), *20*, 24, **73**

Common hackberry (*Celtis occidentalis*), **53**

Common persimmon (*Diospyros virginiana*), **59**

Conifers, 24, 40

Container trees, 33, 35, 37

Cooling by trees, 6, 7

Corkscrew willow (*Salix matsudana* 'Tortuosa'), **85**

Cornus florida, **56**. See Dogwood, flowering

Cornus kousa, **56**. See Kousa dogwood

Crabapple (*Malus*), 16–17, 18, 22, 32, **70**

Crape myrtle (*Lagerstroemia indica*), 16–17, 19, 23, **66**

Crataegus crus-galli (Cockspur hawthorn), **57**

Crataegus phaenopyrum, **57**. See Washington hawthorn

Cryptomeria japonica, **58**. See Japanese cedar

Cupressocyparis × leylandii, **58**. See Leyland cypress

Cupressus sempervirens, **58**. See Italian cypress

D

Davidia involucrata, **59**. See Dove tree

Dawn redwood (*Metasequoia glyptostroboides*), **71**

Deer, 39

Design, 8, 9, 10–13, 23

Diospyros kaki (Japanese persimmon), **59**

Diospyros virginiana (Common persimmon), **59**

Dogwood, flowering (*Cornus florida*), 16–17, 18, *20*, 32, **56**

Dogwood, kousa (*Cornus kousa*). See Kousa dogwood

Douglas fir (*Pseudotsuga menziesii*), 6, **80**

Dove tree (*Davidia involucrata*), 19, **59**

Downy serviceberry (*Amelanchier arborea*), **50**

Dutch elm disease, 91

E

Eastern redbud (*Cercis canadensis*), 18, **54**

Eastern red cedar (*Juniperus virginiana*), 6, **65**

Eastern white pine (*Pinus strobus*), 6, **75**

Elaeagnus angustifolia, **60**. See Russian olive

Elm (*Ulmus*), **91**

Empress tree (*Paulownia tomentosa*), 18, **72**

English holly, 22

English laurel. See Cherry laurel

English oak (*Quercus robur*), 13, 15, **84**

Eriobotrya japonica (Loquat), **61**

Erosion prevention, 6

Eucalyptus, **60–61**. See Gum tree

European beech (*Fagus sylvatica*), 5, 7, 15, *20, 21*, **62**

European black alder (*Alnus glutinosa*), **50**

European hornbeam (*Carpinus betulus*), 11, 13, **52**

European larch (*Larix decidua*), **67**

European mountain ash (*Sorbus aucuparia*), 16–17, 19, 22, **88**

European white birch (*Betula pendula*), **51**

Evergreens, 6, 23, 24–25, 37, 38

F

Fagus grandifolia, **62**. See American beech

Fagus sylvatica, **62**. See European beech

Fall
  appearance of multiseason all-star trees, 16–17
  flowering time, 18–19
  foliage, 21
  planting, 37

Fast-growing trees, 14

Fertilizing, 39, 42

Fire blight, 80–81

Firs (*Abies*), 6, **45**

Five-stamen tamarisk (*Tamarix ramosissima*), 19, **89**

Flood adapted trees, 31

Flowering cherry (*Prunus hybrids*), **79**

Flowering crabapples (*Malus*). See Crabapple

Flowering dogwood (*Cornus florida*). See Dogwood, flowering

Flowering times of trees, 18–19

Foliage, 20, 21, 25

Fragrant snowbell (*Styrax obassia*), **88**

Franklin tree (*Franklinia alatamaha*), 19, **62**

Fraxinus americana (White ash), **63**

Fraxinus pennsylvanica (Green ash), **63**

G

Giant dogwood 'Variegata' (*Cornus controversa*), *20*

Giant sequoia (*Sequoiadendron giganteum*), **87**

Gingko (*Gingko biloba*), *21*, **64**

Gleditsia triacanthos var. *inermis*, **64**. See also Thornless honeylocust

Goldenchain tree (*Laburnum × watereri*), 5, 18, 19, **66**

Golden larch (*Pseudolarix amabilis (kaempferi)*), **80**

Goldenrain tree (*Koelreuteria paniculata*), 19, 22, **66**

Golden weeping willow (*Salix alba* var. *tristis*), **85**

Grade levels, changing, 43

Green ash (*Fraxinus pennsylvanica*), **63**

Growing trees. See specific tree species

Growth rate, 14. See specific tree species

Gum tree (*Eucalyptus*), 7, 15, **60–61**

H

Hackberry, common (*Celtis occidentalis*), **53**

Halesia tetraptera, **64**. See Carolina silverbell

Hardiness zones, 26, 27

Hawthorn (*Crataegus*), 16–17, 19, **57**

Hemlock. See Canadian hemlock

Higan cherry (*Prunus subhirtella*), 18, **78–79**

Holly, American (*Ilex opaca*), **65**

Honeylocust. See Thornless honeylocust

Hornbeam, **52**. See European hornbeam

Horsechestnut, common (*Aesculus hippocastanum*), 7, 15, 18, **49**

Horsechestnut, red (*Aesculus × carnea*), 18, 19, **49**

I

Ilex opaca (American holly), **65**

Italian cypress (*Cupressus sempervirens*), 13, **58**

Italian stone pine (*Pinus pinea*), **74**

J

Japanese black pine (*Pinus thunbergii*), **75**

Japanese cedar (*Cryptomeria japonica*), 6, **58**

Japanese flowering cherry (*Prunus serrulata*), 16–17, 18

Japanese larch (*Larix kaempferi*), **67**

Japanese maple (*Acer palmatum*), 5, 10, 13, 16–17, 21, 32, 44, **47**

Japanese pagoda tree (*Sophora japonica*), 6, 19, **87**

Japanese persimmon (*Diospyros kaki*), **59**

Japanese red pine (*Pinus densiflora*), **74**

Japanese snowbell (*Styrax japonicus*), 19, **88**

Japanese stewartia (*Stewartia pseudocamellia*), 19, 23, **88**

Japanese tree lilac (*Syringa reticulata*), 19, **89**

Japanese umbrella pine (*Sciadopitys verticillata*), **87**

Japanese zelkova (*Zelkova serrata*), **92**

Juglans nigra (Black walnut), **65**
Juniperus virginiana (Eastern red cedar), 6, **65**

K

Katsura tree (*Cercidiphyllum japonicum*), *42*, **54**
Koelreuteria paniculata, **66**. See Goldenrain tree
Korean mountain ash (*Sorbus alnifolia*), **88**
Korean stewartia (*Stewartia pseudocamellia* 'Korean Beauty'), 5, 16–17
Kousa dogwood (*Cornus kousa*), 16–17, 19, *20*, *22*, *23*, **56**

L

Laburnum × *watereri*, **66.** See Goldenchain tree
Lacebark elm. See Chinese elm
Lacebark pine, 23
Lagerstroemia indica, **66**. See Crape myrtle
Larch, *21*, **67**
    European, **67**
    golden, **80**
    Japanese, **67**
Larix kaempferi, **67**. See Japanese larch
Lawson false cypress (*Chamaecyparis lawsoniana*), **54**
Leaf miner, 57
Lemon bottlebrush (*Callistemon citrinus*), **52**
Lemon gum (*Eucalyptus citriodora*), **60**
Leyland cypress (*Cupressocyparis* × *leylandii*), 6, **58**
Light, and tree location, 29
Linden (*Tilia*), 7, **90**
Liquidambar styraciflua, **67**. See Sweet gum
Liriodendron tulipifera, **67**. See Tulip tree
Littleleaf linden (*Tilia cordata*), **90**
Live oak (*Quercus agrifolia*), 15, **82**
Location, 7, 26–33, 44. See specific tree species
London plane tree (*Platanus* × *acerifolia*), 7, 15, **76**
Longevity, 15
Loquat (*Eriobotrya japonica*), **61**

M

Magnolia grandiflora, **68**. See Southern magnolia
Magnolia macrophylla, **68**. See Bigleaf magnolia
Magnolia stellata (Star magnolia), **69**
Magnolia virginiana (Sweet bay magnolia), **69**
Magnolia × *soulangiana*, **69**. See Saucer magnolia
Mail-order sources, 93
Malus, **70**. See Crabapple
Maples (*Acer* spp.). See specific species
Mescal bean (*Sophora secundiflora*), **87**
Metasequoia glyptostroboides (Dawn redwood), **71**
Microclimates, 30
Mimosa webworm, 64
Mites, 45, 73
Monterey cypress (*Cupressus macrocarpa*), *31*, **58**
Mountain silverbell (*Halesia monticola*), **64**
Mulching, 39
Myrobalan plum. See Cherry plum

N

National Arbor Day Foundation, 5, 42
Needled evergreen trees, 24–25
Nitrogen, 6, 28
Noble fir (*Abies procera*), **45**
Noise reduction, 6
Nordmann fir (*Abies nordmanniana*), **45**
Northern catalpa (*Catalpa speciosa*), **53**
Northern red oak (*Quercus rubra*). See Red oak
Norway maple (*Acer platanoides*), 7, 20, **47**
Norway spruce (*Picea abies*), 6, **73**
Nyssa sylvatica, **71**. See Black gum

O

Oaks (*Quercus*), **82–84**. See specific species
Ohio buckeye (*Aesculus glabra*), **49**
Olive (*Olea europaea*), **71**
Oriental persimmon. See Japanese persimmon
Oriental spruce (*Picea orientalis*), **73**
Oxydendrum arboreum, **72.** See Sourwood

P

Paperbark cherry, 23
Paperbark maple (*Acer griseum*), 23, 32, **46**
Paper birch (*Betula papyrifera*), 23, 44, **51**
Paulownia tomentosa (Empress tree), 18, **72**
Pawpaw (*Asimina triloba*), **51**
Pear (*Pyrus*), **81**. See Callery pear
Pecan (*Carya illinoinensis*), **52**
Pepper tree (*Schinus molle*), 32, **86**
Persimmon, common (*Diospyros virginiana*), **59**
pH, soil, 28
Phellodendron amurense (Amur cork tree), **72**
Phosphorus, 28, 37
Picea abies (Norway spruce), 6, **73**
Picea orientalis (Oriental spruce), **73**
Picea pungens glauca, **73**. See Colorado blue spruce
Pin oak (*Quercus palustris*), **83**
Pinus densiflora (Japanese red pine), **74**
Pinus nigra (Austrian pine), 6, **74**
Pinus pinea (Italian stone pine), **74**
Pinus strobus (Eastern white pine), 6, **75**
Pinus sylvestris, **75**. See Scotch pine
Pinus thunbergii (Japanese black pine), **75**
Pistacia chinensis (Chinese pistachio), **76**
Planting, 36–37
Platanus × *acerifolia*, **76**. See London plane tree
Plum, cherry. See Cherry plum
Podocarpus macrophyllus (Yew pine), **76**
Poplar (*Populus*), 32, **77**
    P. alba (White poplar), **77**
    P. tremuloides (Quaking aspen), **77**
Portuguese laurel (*Prunus lusitanica*), **78**
Potassium, 28
Power lines and trees, 32
Property value and trees, 5
Pruning, 36, 40–42. See specific tree species
Prunus cerasifera, **77**. See Cherry plum
Prunus hybrids, **79**. See Cherry, flowering
Prunus laurocerasus (Cherry laurel), **78**
Prunus maackii (Amur chokecherry), **78**
Prunus sargentii, **78**. See Sargent cherry
Pseudocydonia sinensis, **80**. See Chinese quince
Pseudolarix amabilis (Golden larch), **80**

Pseudotsuga menziesii (Douglas fir), 6, **80**
Pyrus calleryana, **81**. See Callery pear
Pyrus salicifolia (Willow-leaved pear), **81**

Q

Quaking aspen (*Populus tremuloides*), **77**
Quercus agrifolia (Coast live oak), **82**
Quercus alba, **82**. See White oak
Quercus imbricaria (Shingle oak), **82**
Quercus macrocarpa (Bur Oak), **83**
Quercus palustris (Pin oak), **83**
Quercus phellos (Willow oak), **83**
Quercus robur (English Oak), **84**
Quercus rubra, **84**. See Red oak

R

Rabbits, 39
Rainfall, 26
Red buckeye (*Aesculus pavia*), **49**
Redbud, eastern (*Cercis canadensis*), 18, **54**
Red-flowering gum (*Eucalyptus ficifolia*), 19, **60**
Red horsechestnut (*Aesculus* × *carnea*), 18, 19, **49**
Red maple (*Acer rubrum*), 7, 16–17, 18, *21*, **48**
Redmond linden (*Tilia* × *flavescens*), 7, **90**
Red oak (*Quercus rubra*), 7, 15, **84**
Redwood (*Sequoia*), 15, **87**
River birch (*Betula nigra*), 15, 23, **51**
Robinia pseudoacacia, **85**. See Black locust
Rocky Mountain fir (*Abies lasiocarpa*), **45**
Rooms, outdoor, 8–9
Roots, 28, 32, 36–37, 42, 43
Russian olive (*Elaeagnus angustifolia*), **60**

S

Salix (Willow), **85**
Salt damage, 42
Sandy soils, trees for, 28
Sapium sebiferum (Chinese tallow tree), **86**
Sargent cherry (*Prunus sargentii*), 15, 16–17, 18, **78**
Sassafras (*Sassafras albidum*), 16–17, 18, **86**
Saucer magnolia (*Magnolia* × *soulangiana*), 18, 33, **69**
Scale, 86
Schinus molle (Pepper tree), 32, **86**
Sciadopitys verticillata (Japanese umbrella pine), **87**
Scotch pine (*Pinus sylvestris*), 6, 23, **75**
Seashore trees, 31
Seasons, 16–19
Sequoia sempervirens (Coast redwood), 15, **87**
Serviceberry (*Amelanchier*), 16–17, 18, **50**
Shade tolerant trees, 7, 29
Shingle oak (*Quercus imbricaria*), **82**
Silk tree (*Albizia julibrissin*), 19, **50**
Silver dollar gum (*Eucalyptus polyanthemos*), **61**
Silver linden (*Tilia tomentosa*), **90**
Silver maple (*Acer saccharinum*), 7, 32, **48**
Silver mountain gum (*Eucalyptus pulverulenta*), **60**
Site selection. See specific tree species
Slopes, trees for, 31
Small-space trees, 32–33
Snow gum (*Eucalyptus pauciflora var. niphophila*), **61**
Soil, 6, 28, 36

Sophora japonica, **87**. See Japanese pagoda tree
Sorbus aucuparia, **88**. See European mountain ash
Sour gum. See Black gum
Sourwood (*Oxydendrum arboreum*), 16–17, *19, 21, 22*, **72**
Southern catalpa (*Catalpa bignonioides*), *19*, **53**
Southern magnolia (*Magnolia grandiflora*), *18, 19*, **68**
Spider mites, 45
Spring
  appearance of multiseason all-star trees, 16–17
  flowering time, 18–19
  planting, 37
Spruce budworm, 45
Spruce (*Picea*), **73**. See Colorado blue spruce
Staking, 38
Star magnolia (*Magnolia stellata*), **69**
Stewartia pseudocamellia, **88**. See Japanese stewartia
Street trees, 31
Styrax japonicus (Japanese snowbell), **88**
Sugar maple (*Acer saccharum*), *7*, **48**
Summer
  appearance of multiseason all-star trees, 16–17
  flowering time, 18–19
  foliage, 20
Sweet bay magnolia (*Magnolia virginiana*), **69**
Sweet gum (*Liquidambar styraciflua*), *7, 32*, **67**
Sycamore maple 'Brilliantisimum' (*Acer pseudoplatanus*), *20*
Sycamore (*Platanus occidentalis*), **76**
Syringa reticulata (Japanese tree lilac), *19*, **89**

T

Tamarix ramosissima (Five-stamen tamarisk), *19*, **89**
Taxodium distichum, **89**. See Bald cypress
Temperature, 26–27
Temporary trees, 14
Thornless honeylocust (*Gleditsia triacanthos* var. *inermis*), *6, 15*, **64**
Thorny elaeagnus (*Elaeagnus pungens*), **60**
Threeflower maple (*Acer triflorum*), **46**
Thuja occidentalis, **90**. See American arborvitae
Tilia cordata (Littleleaf linden), **90**
Tilia tomentosa (Silver linden), **90**
Tingirini gum (*Eucalyptus glauescens*), *20*
Tools, pruning, 40
Traffic, guiding, *8, 9*
Transpiration, 6
Transplanting trees, 35, 37
Transporting trees, 35
Trunks, 38, 39, 43. See also Bark appearance
Tsuga canadensis, **91**. See Canadian hemlock
Tulip tree (*Liriodendron tulipifera*), *7, 15, 21*, **67**
Twig blight, 66

U

Ulmus americana (American Elm), **91**
Ulmus parvifolia (Chinese elm), *23*, **91**
USDA hardiness zone, 26, 27
Utility lines and trees, 32

V

Value of trees, 4–13
View and design, *8, 9*
Vitex agnus-castus (Chaste tree), *19*, **92**

W

Walnut, black (*Juglans nigra*), **65**
Washington hawthorn (*Crataegus phaenopyrum*), *16–17*, **57**
Watering, 36–37, 39, 42
Water sprouts, 40
Weeping trees, *11, 23*, **85**
Weeping willow (*Salix alba*), **85**
Wet-soil-tolerant trees, 28
White ash (*Fraxinus americana*), **63**
White fir (*Abies concolor*), *6*, **45**
White fringe tree (*Chionanthus virginicus*), *18, 19*, **55**
White oak (*Quercus alba*), *7, 15*, **82**
White pine (*Pinus strobus*), **75**
White poplar (*Populus alba*), **77**
Willow-leaved pear (*Pyrus salicifolia*), **81**
Willow oak (*Quercus phellos*), **83**
Willow (*Salix*), *32*, **85**
Windbreaks, *6*, 60
Winter
  appearance of multiseason all-star trees, 16–17
  evergreens, 24
  structure of trees, 23
Winter King hawthorn (*Crataegus viridis* 'Winter King'), 16–17
Woodland garden, 12–13, 31
Wrapping trunks, 38

Y–Z

Yellowwood (*Cladrastis lutea*), *7, 16–17, 18*, **55**
Yew pine (*Podocarpus macrophyllus*), **76**
Zelkova serrata (Japanese zelkova), **92**
Ziziphus jujuba (Chinese date), **92**

METRIC CONVERSIONS

U.S. Units to Metric Equivalents			Metric Units to U.S. Equivalents		
To Convert From	Multiply By	To Get	To Convert From	Multiply By	To Get
Inches	25.4	Millimeters	Millimeters	0.0394	Inches
Inches	2.54	Centimeters	Centimeters	0.3937	Inches
Feet	30.48	Centimeters	Centimeters	0.0328	Feet
Feet	0.3048	Meters	Meters	3.2808	Feet
Yards	0.9144	Meters	Meters	1.0936	Yards
Square inches	6.4516	Square centimeters	Square centimeters	0.1550	Square inches
Square feet	0.0929	Square meters	Square meters	10.764	Square feet
Square yards	0.8361	Square meters	Square meters	1.1960	Square yards
Acres	0.4047	Hectares	Hectares	2.4711	Acres
Cubic inches	16.387	Cubic centimeters	Cubic centimeters	0.0610	Cubic inches
Cubic feet	0.0283	Cubic meters	Cubic meters	35.315	Cubic feet
Cubic feet	28.316	Liters	Liters	0.0353	Cubic feet
Cubic yards	0.7646	Cubic meters	Cubic meters	1.308	Cubic yards
Cubic yards	764.55	Liters	Liters	0.0013	Cubic yards

To convert from degrees Fahrenheit (F) to degrees Celsius (C), first subtract 32, then multiply by ⁵⁄₉.

To convert from degrees Celsius to degrees Fahrenheit, multiply by ⁹⁄₅, then add 32.